The War

for Children's Minds

STEPHEN LAW

The War

for Children's Minds

Routledge
Taylor & Francis Group

LONDON AND NEW YORK

First published 2006 by Routledge
2 Park Square, Milton Park, Abingdon, OX14 4RN

Simultaneously published in the USA and Canada
by Routledge
270 Madison Ave, New York, NY 10016

*Routledge is an imprint of the Taylor & Francis Group,
an informa business*

© 2006 Stephen Law

Typeset in Joanna MT and DIN by Keyword Group Ltd
Printed and bound in Great Britain by MPG Books Ltd, Bodmin

British Library Cataloguing in Publication Data
A catalogue record for this book is available from the British Library

Library of Congress Cataloging in Publication Data

ISBN10: 0-415-37855-9
ISBN10: 0-203-96942-1 (ebk)
ISBN13: 978-0-415-37855-0
ISBN13: 978-0-203-96942-7 (ebk)

For Anoushka

"*Ideas are more powerful than guns. We would not let our enemies have guns, why should we let them have ideas?*"

Joseph Stalin

"*We should always be disposed to believe that which appears to us to be white is really black, if the hierarchy of the church so decides.*"

St Ignatius Loyola

Contents

Acknowledgements

I have received valuable help from the following, to whom I'm most grateful:

Anthony Baxter
Tony Bruce
Tony Carroll
Tom Crowther
Peter Gallagher
Rodas Irving
Aurelian Koch
Michael Lacewing
Marilyn Mason
Richard Norman
Mick O'Neill
Tom Pilling
Patrick Riordan
Jeremy Stangroom
John Storey
Karenza Storey
Taryn Storey
Bridget Gilfillan Upton
Michael Walsh
Nigel Warburton

About Notes and Appendices

This book is written primarily for those with little if any knowledge of philosophy who are interested in the question of how liberal we should be in our approach to moral and religious education. However, I realize these arguments will also be of interest to some more academically-inclined readers who may want more detail than is provided in the main text. Where I have guessed that is the case, I've supplemented the text with endnotes that develop the argument in more depth. If you want to read the endnotes along with the main text, I suggest you read with a finger tucked in the relevant page at the back. Readers who can't be bothered with the endnotes need not worry, however – the main argument is intended to be robust enough to stand on its own.

I have also included two Appendices. Appendix One deals in more detail with the suggestion that the Enlightenment, and more specifically Enlightenment as Kant famously characterized it, was responsible for the Holocaust. Appendix Two looks at the work of the philosopher Alisdair MacIntyre and its relevance to this debate.

Stephen Law has a website at www.thinking-big.co.uk

How do we raise good children? How do we make moral citizens? Most of us find ourselves drawn to one of two traditions when it comes to moral education. These traditions disagree about the kind of attitude we should encourage in the young about morality. One tradition – I'll call it the authoritarian tradition – says that the right attitude is one of *deference to authority*. Should you steal from supermarkets? Is abortion wrong? Are same sex marriages morally acceptable? It's important, says the authoritarian, that you realize that the answers to these questions are not for you to decide. You should consult an appropriate moral authority. A good moral education, according to this tradition, involves getting the young to defer to a higher authority that can determine right and wrong for them.

What sort of authority should it be? Often, it's religious. The authority might be a particular religious book such as *The Koran* or *The Bible*. Or it might be a religious individual: a rabbi or an imam for example. It might be your 'faith community'. It might even be God himself. But secular cultures can be authoritarian too. In a totalitarian communist regime, young people wanting to know the answers to moral questions might be encouraged to defer to their local communist party official.

The other tradition, which I'll call the liberal tradition, insists that people should ultimately make up their own minds about morality. Rather than encouraging them to defer to authority, we should confront young people with their responsibility to think for themselves about right and wrong. A good moral education, on this liberal view, involves making sure new citizens have the skills they need to discharge that responsibility properly.

Of course, moral education can be more or less liberal. There's a sliding scale between the liberal and authoritarian extremes. Not so long ago, most Westerners were morally educated in a fairly authoritarian way. We were simply told what we should and shouldn't believe. Dissent might provoke a rap on the knuckles. Independent critical thought was rarely tolerated, and certainly not encouraged. But then things changed. During the second half of the Twentieth Century, the liberal tradition has been much more in the ascendant. The 1960s, in particular, saw it make huge inroads into Western culture. We were encouraged to liberate ourselves from the old religious authorities and traditions, which were increasingly seen as restrictive and oppressive. More and more emphasis was placed on personal autonomy and freedom of thought and expression.

But as we begin the Twenty-First Century many have begun to look back and wonder whether we didn't go *too* far. Of course, not everyone wants to see a return to the do-and-think-as-you're-told ways of the past. But more and more of us are now voicing the concern that the West has now become *excessively* liberal in the way it raises tomorrow's citizens. Take the huge rise in crime over the last 50 years, the corporate shenanigans, the explosions in unwanted teenage pregnancies and the drug abuse. Consider the rise in delinquency, the prevalence of violent attacks and the breakdown of discipline within schools and families. What these things show, it's argued, is that without the firm moral framework that only authority-based – or at least rather *more* authority-based – approach to moral education can provide, moral chaos is the inevitable result. There's an emerging consensus that the West faces a moral crisis brought about by Enlightenment- and 1960s-inspired liberalism, and that it's time to redress the balance. In 1996 a Gallup poll indicated that three quarters of the UK population believed both that society was less moral than it was 50 years previously, and that too much moral choice is left to individuals.[1]

This diagnosis of where we went wrong unites many otherwise highly diverse individuals. That the West is now rather *too* liberal is one of the few things that a left-leaning politician like Tony Blair, a right-wing US neo-conservative like Irving Kristol, an Islamic terrorist supporter like Osama bin Laden and a moderate cleric like the Archbishop of Canterbury can probably all agree on. Across the globe, the pendulum is beginning to swing back in the direction of authority. In many parts of America, 'liberal' is now a dirty word.[2]

This book is about the ongoing debate between these two opposing traditions. Just how do we raise good people? Just how liberal, or how authoritarian, should we be? Parents, teachers and policymakers constantly find themselves confronted by this question. On the one hand, many of us seem embarrassed even to bring up the subject of morality with our offspring. Certainly, many are no longer confident about saying 'Do as you are told' or 'I know best'. On the other hand, most of us fear that, if we give up on telling children what to think and do, they'll grow up morally rudderless.

So what's the answer? This book defends an increasingly unfashionable position. It argues that we should be *very liberal indeed* in our approach to moral education. It makes a case for a particular kind of liberal moral education, an education rooted in philosophy, not authority.

Whether or not you end up agreeing with the main thrust of the book, my hope is that it will provide you with an essential pocket-guide to the many ideas and arguments, new and old, about how to raise good citizens. It's a book, in particular, for those parents, teachers and policymakers who are now being bombarded with a great deal of conflicting, muddled and sometimes downright silly advice. It should, at the very least, help them make a far more informed and confident choice.

One

The Age of Enlightenment

The kind of liberal approach to moral education argued for here has its roots in an intellectual movement that stretches from the Seventeenth Century to the beginning of the Nineteenth Century, a movement known as the Enlightenment. This chapter sets the scene for the argument that follows by explaining the pivotal role that the Enlightenment is commonly supposed to have had in shaping our current moral climate. In particular, we will see why the Enlightenment is commonly thought to be the root cause of many of today's social problems – why it's claimed that *we're now living with the Enlightenment's 'twisted legacy'* (Phillips 1998: 233).

The term 'Enlightenment' was intended to contrast the new 'Age of Reason' with the darkness of the middle ages, which were supposedly dominated by irrationality and superstition, authority and tradition. Prior to the Enlightenment, education very largely took the form of the handing down of truths by received authorities. This was particularly true of moral education. Children, and even adults, were expected to accept, more or less uncritically, the moral pronouncements of religious authority.

The Enlightenment revolutionized Europe both intellectually and politically. One of the most revolutionary features of the Enlightenment was the vigorous way in which philosophers and other thinkers began to scrutinize, and sometimes reject, the pronouncements of religious and other authorities. They started to place far more importance on the individual and his or her powers of reason. The French intellectuals Diderot and d'Alembert defined the Enlightenment thinker as one who,

> trampling on prejudice, tradition, universal consent, authority, in a word, all that enslaves most minds, dares to *think for himself* (Phillips 1998: 190; emphasis added).

Daring to think for yourself is a core Enlightenment value. As we'll see, it was with the dramatic rise of this value that the seeds of our current 'moral malaise' were supposedly sown.

Galileo's Telescope

The Seventeenth Century astronomer Galileo was an important figure in the run up to the Enlightenment, and he nicely illustrates this core value in action. For centuries the Catholic Church had taught that the Earth is fixed at the centre of the universe. This belief was backed up by the Bible – which says that the Earth is fixed and immovable – and by the teaching of the Ancient Greek philosopher Aristotle, who, along with the Bible, was the source of most of the Church's scientific and cosmological beliefs at that time. Aristotle taught that all heavenly bodies revolve around a stationary Earth.

In 1632, Galileo started to question this traditional model of the universe. He developed a telescope through which he could observe the heavens in more detail. Galileo's telescope revealed that the planet Jupiter had moons that slowly revolved around it. By daring to use his own eyes and his own understanding, Galileo revealed powerful evidence that Aristotle was wrong: not everything revolved around the Earth. Galileo eventually came to accept the Copernican model on which the Earth moved about the sun, not vice versa.

What was the reaction of Church Authority to Galileo's independence of thought? He was intimidated into retracting his theory. When Galileo was alleged to have again claimed his theory was literally true, the Inquisition showed him the instruments of torture and imprisoned him for life (the sentence was later reduced to permanent house arrest).

Galileo got off comparatively lightly: his friend Giordano Bruno was burnt at the stake for daring to voice similarly heretical views. But of course, Enlightenment thinkers eventually won this particular battle with the Church. By daring to trust their own intelligence and figure things out for themselves, they finally succeeded in throwing off an authoritarian straightjacket that had for hundreds of years stifled man's attempts to understand the world around him. By so doing, they gave birth to modern science.

Kant on Enlightenment

Enlightenment is also about daring to think for yourself on *moral* issues. A key figure here is Immanuel Kant, perhaps the greatest of all the Enlightenment philosophers. Kant locates the responsibility for making moral judgements, not in some external authority or tradition, but in the individual. Individuals should dare to apply their own powers of reason and make their *own* moral judgement rather than defer to some external authority (such as their imam, rabbi or the Pope).

In fact, Kant didn't just believe that each individual should make their own judgement, he also thought that pure reason, applied independently of any external authority or tradition, can provide the individual with a firm moral foundation. Kant thought that, when it comes to determining right and wrong, *reason is all you need* (clearly, this is a much stronger, and rather more controversial, claim than the claim that individuals ought to think for themselves and make their own judgements).

In 1784, Kant wrote a short magazine article entitled 'What is Enlightenment?'. Kant, not normally known for his brevity, came up with one of the most quoted characterizations of Enlightenment:

[Enlightenment is the] emergence of man from his self-imposed infancy. Infancy is the inability to use one's reason without the guidance of another. It is self-imposed, when it depends on a deficiency, not of reason, but of the resolve and courage to use it without external guidance. Thus the watchword of enlightenment is: *Sapere aude!* Have the courage to use one's own reason! (Kant, quoted in the entry on 'Enlightenment' in the *Oxford Companion to Philosophy* 1995).

This book is, in effect, a defence of Kant's Enlightenment vision of a society of morally autonomous individuals who dare to apply their own intelligence rather than more-or-less uncritically accept the pronouncements of authority.

Two Kinds of 'Enlightenment'

We need to be careful what we mean by 'Enlightenment', for at least two things go by that name.

First, there is Enlightenment as Kant characterizes it above. Notice that Kant's characterization is of something like a *state of mind*. If you're an Enlightened individual, in Kant's sense, then you are not cowed and afraid, mindlessly accepting the pronouncements of tradition and authority. You are courageous: you dare to apply your own powers of reason; you dare to think for yourself. Indeed, Kant believes each of us is morally 'autonomous' in the sense that we ultimately *must* take on the responsibility for making moral judgements. That duty is unavoidable. The Enlightened individual is one who recognizes this.

Secondly, there is the Enlightenment – the historical, intellectual movement. The boundaries of this movement are not precise. There is a whole raft of beliefs associated to varying degrees with the Enlightenment, and in characterizing the Enlightenment different commentators tend to put the emphasis in different places and on different individuals.[1] Of course, not everything about the Enlightenment was noble, and not every Enlightenment thought was true. For example, some Enlightenment philosophers believed that through the application of reason progress would be inevitable – indeed, some supposed that all mankind's fundamental problems would finally be solved. In retrospect that seems ridiculously naïve.

Other Enlightenment thinkers believed that morality could be given a *wholly* rational foundation (as we've just seen, that's Kant's view). In fact some contemporary thinkers, such as MacIntyre (1985) and Gray (1995a: 147), maintain that giving morality a wholly rational foundation was the core 'Enlightenment project'.

One reason why it's important not to conflate these two senses of 'Enlightenment' is that there may be valid criticisms of the Enlightenment that are not valid criticisms of Enlightenment as Kant characterizes it. One of the most popular criticisms of the Enlightenment – a criticism made by MacIntyre and Gray, for example – is that *the core 'Enlightenment project' of providing morality with a foundation in reason alone had inevitably to fail*. Morality cannot be rationally underpinned in the way the Enlightenment philosophers thought. But then, because the Enlightenment had kicked away the old moral foundations of tradition and authority, it left morality *without any foundations at all*. And so, as a direct consequence of the Enlightenment, morality began to collapse.

This is a serious charge. But whether or not it's a cogent criticism of the Enlightenment, notice that we can still sign up to Kant's Enlightenment vision – we can still agree on the importance of getting individuals to think and judge independently rather than defer to a religious authority – even while admitting that morality cannot be given a *wholly* rational foundation. This is a point I will be exploring in more detail later (especially in chapter nine and the appendix on MacIntyre). But it's worth clarifying at the outset that *when this book speaks of the importance of Enlightenment, it's talking specifically about what Kant means by 'Enlightenment'*.

Modern Critics of Enlightenment

Enlightenment, as Kant characterizes it, is increasingly viewed with suspicion. It's claimed that the rise of Kantian Enlightenment in the West has resulted in the undermining of external moral authority and its replacement by individual moral autonomy. This in turn has resulted in the collapse of morality itself, with all the attendant anti-social consequences we see around us today: the escalation in crime and delinquency; sexual irresponsibility and the rise in single parent families; a greedy, self-serving, individualistic culture. According to many social commentators, as a direct result of Kant's Enlightenment vision, the fabric of Western civilization is now under threat. As one well-known British journalist puts it,

> [t]he great paradox of the Enlightenment was that, in liberating human thought in order to enhance civilization, it lit a slow fuse beneath it (Phillips 1998: 197).

Jonathan Sacks, the UK's Chief Rabbi, is another of those who believe that the Enlightenment and, in particular, Kant's Enlightenment vision is the fundamental cause of many of today's social problems. Sacks (1997: 176) comes down particularly hard on Kant, whose view he sums up like so:

> [A]ccording to Kant ... [t]o do something because others do, or because of habit or custom or even Divine Command, is to accept an external authority over the one sovereign territory that is truly our own: our own choices. The moral being for Kant is by definition an autonomous being, a person who accepts no other authority than the self. By the 1960s this was beginning to gain hold as an educational orthodoxy. The task of education is not to hand on a tradition but to enhance the consciousness of choice.

Sacks rejects Kant's insistence on individual moral autonomy. He claims that once Kant's idea that each individual was morally autonomous caught hold in schools and colleges, the seeds of our current moral calamity were sown. For morality was then reduced to a mere personal 'preference' or 'choice'. The cure, Sacks argues, requires that we move back in the direction of external religious authority and tradition.

You'll also find within Sacks' writings another popular refrain: that contemporary society is dangerously fragmented and individualistic. It's all very well encouraging individuals to think independently, but the result of promoting Kant's view that the moral being is, as Sacks puts it, 'an autonomous being, a person who accepts no other authority than the self', is an atomized society of free-floating individuals. Once we lose our anchor in one of the great, shared religious traditions we are left morally all at sea, with no way of telling right from wrong other than how we happen to feel. Moral chaos is the inevitable result. We need to return to those faith traditions and authorities that once wove us together into moral communities and provided us with a moral compass.

While it's usually left-leaning liberals that get the blame for the moral malaise, Sacks is clear that the cultural movement he takes himself to be attacking is not uniquely politically left-of-centre. The right's enthusiasm for selfish individualism also bears some responsibility. The individualistic 'greed is good' mentality of the 1980s is supposedly yet another legacy of the Enlightenment's insistence on individual autonomy.

Enlightenment has always had its critics, and the kinds of criticisms levelled by Sacks are not new. But these criticisms are now being taken much more seriously, and are beginning to impact on policy. The UK government's enthusiasm for faith schools would seem to be one manifestation of this trend.

In fact, some counter-Enlightenment thinkers go so far as to suggest that the West is now in the grip of a full-blown 'culture war' between, on the one hand, liberal defenders of Kant's Enlightenment vision of a society of morally autonomous individuals, and, on the other, those who wish for a return to traditional Judeo-Christian values and authority-based moral education. Many of these culture war theorists warn we are teetering on the edge of disaster. They write books with panicky titles like *On Looking into the Abyss* (Himmelfarb 1994) and *The Death of Right and Wrong* (Bruce 2003). Unless action is taken quickly to rehabilitate traditional (that's to say, religious) sources of moral authority, the West is likely to become a moral wasteland. Moral and religious education is, of course, at the front line in this culture war. Indeed, as these culture war theorists see it, their war is, above all, a war for children's minds.

Islam and Enlightenment

It's not just Westerners who are urging us to move back in the direction of religious tradition and authority. You'll hear dire warnings of our moral rot coming from non-Westerners too. The 'blame it on Enlightenment' diagnosis is particularly popular in the Islamic world.

Unlike the West, Islam never really experienced a full-blown Enlightenment of its own (which is not to say it has not had Enlightened thinkers, nor to deny its contribution towards Western Enlightenment[2]). Muslim countries still tend to be dominated by religious authority. The Kantian idea that individuals should think independently and make their own moral judgements is widely frowned upon. The questioning of religious belief is strongly discouraged – indeed, it's rarely tolerated, even within an academic setting. To reject the Islamic belief system within which you were raised is, in many places, to risk your life. In Saudi Arabia, Qatar, Yemen, Iran, Sudan, Pakistan and Mauritania, those whose independence of thought has led them publicly to cast off the Muslim faith are liable to be executed.

But, even in supposedly secular Islamic states, the power of Islamic religious authorities to gag dissenting individuals is immense. A colleague working in the humanities at a university in a non-theocratic Arab state tells me that she would certainly face censure, and would probably lose her job, were she to arrange a conference at which religious ideas were open to criticism.

And yet these restrictions on freedom of thought and expression are perceived by many Muslims to be a good thing. They justify it by pointing to the West's moral malaise. 'See?' they say. '*That's* what happens when you allow people to turn their back on religious authority.'

Blame it on the Sixties

While some social commentators and academics suggest that the Enlightenment is ultimately to blame for the West's moral decline, it's a more recent period that tends to bear responsibility in the public imagination: the 1960s. The 1960s was a time when Kant's core Enlightenment value of daring to question authority and think for yourself came still more powerfully to the fore. It's precisely this feature of 1960s thinking that many now blame for our current moral meltdown.

Here, for example, is the US neoconservative D'Souza putting his finger on precisely what, from the conservative point of view, was wrong with the 1960s.

> Before the sixties, most Americans believed in a universal moral order that is external to us, that makes demands on us. Our obligation was to conform to that moral order. Earlier generations, right up to the 'greatest generation' of WWII, took for granted this moral order and its commandments. [...] But, beginning in the sixties, several factions – the antiwar movement, the feminist movement, the gay activist movement, and so on – attacked that moral consensus as narrow and oppressive. They fought for a new ethic that would be based *not on external authority but on the sovereignty of the inner self* (emphasis added).

It is, above all, this championing of Kant's Enlightenment ideal – getting individuals to question external authority and think and judge autonomously – that conservatives like D'Souza find fundamentally unacceptable about 1960s thinking.

The 1960s have always been attacked by conservatives. But now it's not just conservatives who point the finger of blame. There's hardly a week goes by that some political pundit doesn't lay responsibility for the West's alleged moral decline on the anti-authoritarian attitudes of 1960s hippies and liberals.

The Return of Young-Earth Creationism

Another illustration of this general counter-Enlightenment drift is provided by the extraordinary rise in the US of the young-Earth creationists, who believe that we should defer to the authority of *The Bible*, not just on moral matters, but on scientific matters too. Genesis says that God made the earth and all species of living thing in just six days, so that's what young-Earth creationists believe, despite the overwhelming scientific evidence to the contrary. They also suppose that, rather than being billions of years old, the universe must have been created sometime in the last 10,000 years (probably about 6000 years ago).

Fifty years ago, the young-Earth creationists were a tiny, uninfluential band of devotees. Polls indicate they now constitute a sizeable proportion of the American public. It would appear that a third or more of Americans defer to the authority of The Bible on the age of the universe and the way in which life appeared on Earth. It's not just on moral matters that The Bible is held to be absolutely authoritative. It's considered equally authoritative on scientific matters as well.[3]

Young-Earth creationism is not solely the preserve of the ill-educated. Many college graduates are drawn to it. A Tennessee academic who recently surveyed his own students writes that scientists like himself are having to fight

> the battles of the Enlightenment all over again. Medieval ideas
> that were killed stone dead by the rise of science three to four
> hundred years ago are not merely twitching; they are alive
> and well in our schools, colleges and universities (*The Guardian*
> 2001: 14).

These medieval ideas are also taking root again *outside* the US. I recently gave a talk on the origin of the universe to the 12- to 14-year-old pupils of a London comprehensive school. My audience seemed strangely reserved. When asked what was wrong, they explained that they simply didn't accept what I was telling them about the Big Bang. About two thirds of them, it turned out, were convinced that the Biblical account of creation was literally true. These south London children genuinely believed that Adam and Eve roamed the garden of Eden along with the dinosaurs just a few thousand years ago. From where had they got these bizarre ideas? From a local evangelical church with strong US links.

Because of the evangelism of American Bible-literalists, young-Earth creationism is on the rise around the world. Russia and Eastern Europe, in particular, are heavily targeted by Christian fundamentalists for whom states newly liberated from communism promise a new frontier in their global 'culture war'. In 2004, the Serbian education minister Ljiljana Colic succeeded (if only temporarily) in removing the teaching of evolution from all state schools, replacing it with the teaching of young-Earth creationism instead.

Defending Kant's Enlightenment Vision

Of course not every opponent of Kant's Enlightenment vision is a religious fanatic. Some are only mildly critical. They couch their resistance to Enlightenment and their enthusiasm for tradition and authority in qualified, measured terms. They say, 'Of course people should think for themselves!' But then, fearing the moral disaster they think may ensue, they quickly follow this up with '… but not too early. And not too much. Let's leave some room for authority and tradition!'

This book argues that there really is no good case for rejecting the principle that, particularly when it comes to making moral judgements, individuals should be raised and educated to question and think critically and independently rather than defer more-or-less uncritically to external authority. It argues for the increasingly unfashionable view that we should be very liberal indeed in our approach to moral education. Far from being of mere historical interest, the global battle for Enlightenment, as Kant characterizes it, is still well and truly on. This is a moment when those of us who believe in Enlightenment need to stand up and argue vigorously in its defence.

Two

Freedom of Action

Let's begin by clarifying what it is that divides 'liberals' and 'authoritarians'.

Should children and young people be free to *do* just whatever they want? Of course not. Outside of a few hippy communes, no one believes children, or adults for that matter, should be given complete freedom of action. Everyone thinks there should be at least *some* rules. Just how restrictive these rules are, and just how aggressively they should be enforced, is one of the issues that divides 'liberals' and 'authoritarians'. Many believe that, particularly over the last 50 years or so, we've moved too far up the liberal end of the scale. We've become excessively permissive. The time has come to redress the balance – to move back in the authoritarian direction. They may be right about that.

Freedom of Thought

But there's another, rather different, way in which we can distinguish between 'liberals' and 'authoritarians'. The issue here is freedom of *thought and expression*. To what extent should children be encouraged to *think* for themselves and make their own judgements? To what extent should they be allowed publicly to disagree, to express their own opinions? In particular, to what extent should they be allowed to think critically and question what they're told about right and wrong?

Here too, opinion is divided. But notice that those who are pretty authoritarian on the freedom of action scale might turn out to be fairly liberal on the freedom of thought scale. It's one thing to prohibit doing so-and-so. It's quite another to prohibit people from thinking, saying or arguing that they should be allowed to do so-and-so.

We can represent the freedom of action scale like so:

This scale ranges from total hands-off anarchy at the top, where there are no rules or discipline at all, to an extremely regimented, boot-camp-style regime at the bottom, where strict rules govern every last detail of the child's life, right down to how they part their hair.

Let's now add the freedom of thought scale like so:

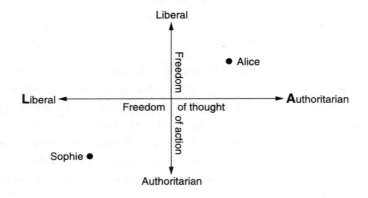

To reduce confusion, when the issue is freedom of thought, let's spell 'Liberal' and 'Authoritarian' with capital initials. Let's call someone 'Authoritarian' if they believe we should place more emphasis on more-or-less-uncritical deference to Authority rather than on independent critical thought. The Authoritarians are over on the right. By a 'Liberal' let's mean someone who thinks we should place the greater emphasis on independent critical thought and freedom of expression. They're to the left.

You can now see that there are four possible combinations of Liberal, liberal, Authoritarian and authoritarian.

It's possible, for example, to be liberal with a small 'l', yet rather Authoritarian with a capital 'A'. Take Alice, a parent who merrily tolerates all sorts of bad behaviour from her children, yet smacks them hard if they ever dare to question the religious faith in which they have been raised. Alice may be pretty liberal with a small 'l', but, at least when it comes to her religion, she's pretty Authoritarian with a capital 'A'. Alice is in the top right quadrant of our chart.

Or take Sophie, who imposes a strict set of rules on her daughters. She expects them to tidy their rooms, do as they're told, and be in bed by nine o'clock sharp. Sophie's pretty authoritarian with a small 'a'. But still, she wants her children to think for themselves. Sophie encourages her daughters to question her rules if they think them unfair. Her attitude is: 'I want you to do what I tell you. But that doesn't mean you have to agree with me. I'm not telling you what you should think. And I'm willing to listen to you and discuss things with you, even if I don't end up agreeing with you.' While Sophie is fairly authoritarian, she's also very Liberal – she's in the bottom left corner of our chart.

The Enlightenment thinkers tended to be very Liberal with a capital 'L'. They encouraged people to think for themselves – to make their own judgements rather than uncritically defer to Authority. That doesn't mean they all thought people should be free to do just whatever they want (few, if any, have ever thought that). Take Kant for example. Kant may have believed in the absolute autonomy of the individual when it comes to moral judgement. But he didn't think individuals should be 'autonomous' in the sense that they should be free to do whatever they feel like. It's worth remembering that Kant, an arch-Liberal, favoured the death penalty for murder.

The question with which we're fundamentally concerned here is: just how Liberal or Authoritarian should we be when it comes to moral education? (Notice we'll be looking at religious education too, because it is so tied up with the teaching of morality: in many cases an individual's religious education is their moral education.) This book argues that, whatever our views on rules and discipline, we should be much more Liberal than Authoritarian. That's to say, *wherever we are on the vertical scale, we should be well to the left, and certainly not to the right, on the horizontal scale.*

Two Schools

Critics often assume Liberals must favour giving up on moral education, abandoning the young to conjure up their own morality out of thin air (we'll see an example of this sort of accusation later[1]). 'Your suggestion that we encourage children, to think for themselves rather than to defer to some external Authority, they say, 'means *casting children into a moral vacuum, leaving them entirely to their own devices, morally speaking, without any moral guidance at all.* It's hardly surprising if they grow up moral degenerates!'

But that is not what is being advocated here. To see why, consider two schools: Liberalia High and Authoritia High. In many respects, these two schools are the same. Both raise their pupils within a clear, firm framework of rules. Both expect pupils to treat teachers and each other with respect, not to run in the corridors, and so on. Both punish pupils when they break the rules. Both also aim to impart a clear set of moral values. But while both schools favour rules and discipline and teach the same moral code, they differ in the kind of attitude they encourage in their students towards those rules and that morality.

Liberalia High is very Liberal. Its pupils are given plenty of opportunity to discuss the rules and regulations that bind them. They're positively encouraged to give their views, particularly if they feel the system is unfair. There's a weekly forum designed to allow

The War for Children's Minds

students to express their opinions to the staff. At the end of the day, it's the head teacher who makes the decisions. But the views of the pupils are heard and taken seriously.

Moral education at Liberalia High is also Liberal. While Liberalia's teachers argue passionately for a particular moral code, they don't expect their pupils to accept that code without question. Walk into a moral education class and you'll hear open debate and frank exchanges of opinion. Dissenting points of view are carefully considered. Teachers feel obliged to answer the questions they are asked honestly and openly – to give reasons, to argue their case. At Liberalia High, the teachers pride themselves on fostering the intellectual and emotional skills pupils need if they are to think critically and independently.

Authoritia High is rather different. While it has the same rules and promotes much the same moral code, its students are not given any opportunity critically to discuss them. Unlike Liberalia High, it expects, not just conformity of behaviour, but conformity of belief. Teachers don't just say, 'Do what you're told to do'; they add '… and think what you're told to think as well!' Moral education at Authoritia High largely takes the form of pronouncements from the teacher about what is right and what is wrong. Questioning of these edicts is not tolerated. If a pupil raises a hand to ask why they should believe that so-and-so is wrong, they'll receive a firm, dismissive put-down. If they persist, they may find themselves in detention or worse.

Clearly, while both schools aim to impart much the same moral code, one is highly Liberal and the other highly Authoritarian. The point I want to extract from this illustration is that a Liberal school is just as free to teach a particular set of moral values as an Authoritarian one. A Liberal approach to moral education *does not require that we gag teachers and prevent them from expressing or promoting any moral point of view* (despite what some critics suggest).

Religious Liberals

Another widespread misconception about the Liberal approach, touched on above, is that it's somehow incompatible with a religious upbringing. Christians, for example, will rightly want to teach their children about the life of Jesus and the kind of morality he represents. Muslims will want to teach their children about the Prophet and the wisdom they believe is embedded in the Koran. As Liberals, they're free to do that.

Again, the difference between, for example, an Authoritarian Christian and a Liberal Christian lies not in what they teach children about Christianity, but in how they teach it. The Authoritarian will expect the child to embrace Christian beliefs more or less on the say-so of a religious Authority. The Liberal Christian, on the other hand, will certainly tolerate, and may even actively encourage, critical scrutiny of religious beliefs.

So while this book argues for a Liberal approach to moral education – while it attacks Authority-based methods of moral education – that's not to say that it's against religion or religious education.

Just so we're clear, however, it's worth spelling out exactly what's required if religious education is to be Liberal. Some religious schools may be under the false impression that they're Liberal.

Suppose the head of a Christian school says, 'But *of course* we allow our pupils to question and critically discuss things – come to one of our Bible study classes and you'll find a very lively discussion going on!' Is this school a Liberal school?

Not necessarily. If it's implicitly communicated to students that their 'lively discussion' is to be kept within the confines of clarifying what they are expected to believe, not whether it should be believed – if it's subtly made clear that asking what Jesus meant is fine, but questions about his existence, divinity, or the truth of what he said are not to be pursued (this must all be accepted without question) – then this school remains pretty Authoritarian. A genuinely Liberal school would not attempt to straight jacket thought in that way.

Atheist Authoritarians

Just as some assume all religious believers must be Authoritarian, so others make the mistake of assuming all atheists must be Liberal. In *Arguing for Atheism*, philosopher Le Poidevin (1996: 84) nicely sets out the positions at the extreme Liberal and Authoritarian ends of the scale like so:

> Compare these two desires: the desire to subordinate oneself utterly to the wishes of some authority ... and the desire that one's behaviour should reflect one's own ideals, to act because one thinks it is right, independently of the will of any other individual. Which is the better ideal, as far as our moral development is concerned? The atheist insists the second desire is the better one. For the atheist the moral ideal is autonomy, or self government. The truly moral agent is one who wishes to be his own master, not the instrument of some other power, and not to trust the deliverances of some supposed authority, but to work out for themselves the rightness of certain kinds of morality.

Le Poidevin much prefers the Liberal desire, and rightly so. But he also assumes that an atheist will be an Enlightened individual. That's a mistake. Atheists can be Authoritarian too, as many totalitarian regimes demonstrate. The party member or worker who sees herself as a mere cog in the great machine of society, who blindly and faithfully accepts what she is told, who dares never to hold or venture any opinion other than that which has been officially endorsed, may have a mind no less enslaved and ruled by Authority than that of a hardline religious zealot.

Authoritarian atheist regimes can also be just as brutal in expunging unacceptable beliefs. In Stalinist Russia, the feared knock on the door in the middle of the night would come, not from the Holy Inquisition hunting down religious heretics, but from the secret police hunting political heretics. What both regimes had in common was an Authoritarian obsession with controlling, not just action, but thought.

We can represent the various possible combinations of Liberal, Authoritarian, religious and atheist by means of a diagram (overleaf):

The Liberal/Authoritarian scale runs left to right. The religious are the top and the atheists at the bottom.

In the top right hand corner you'll find religious Authoritarians. Some Catholics consider the Pope to be the ultimate religious Authority. While the Pope may not be treated as an infallible

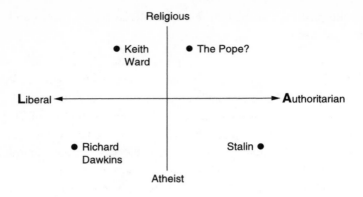

Authority by all his followers (many Catholics openly disagree with him on birth control), still, there are those who believe that, when it comes to matters of faith, the duty of any Catholic is to defer to His Holiness, rather than rely on their own judgement (this may even be the current Pope's view[2]). The following, for example, is from the on-line *Catholic Encyclopedia*'s entry on 'infallibility'.

> [O]ne must listen to the voice of those whom God has expressly appointed to teach in His name, rather than to one's own private judgement in deciding what God's teaching ought to be ... he who chooses to make himself, instead of the authority which God has instituted, the final arbiter in matters of faith is far from possessing the true spirit of faith.[3]

In the bottom right corner you will find Joe Stalin – a brutally Authoritarian atheist prepared to murder anyone brave enough publicly to disagree with him. Over in the top left hand corner are the religious Liberals – they believe in God, but they also believe that each individual must judge for him or herself what is right and what is wrong. When I presented this little chart to Keith Ward, former Professor of Divinity at the University of Oxford, he located himself in the top left hand quadrant (though he did emphasize that he isn't on the *extreme* left of my chart). Ward is a religious Liberal. Finally, in the bottom left corner, you'll find the Liberal atheists.

There are regular public spats between those at the top and bottom of the chart. Richard Dawkins is an atheist well-known for his provocative attacks on religion. His criticisms frequently outrage believers. Dawkins is often accused of having misunderstood them. What is true is that what Dawkins attacks is typically a highly *Authoritarian* brand of religion. Dawkins tends to focus his attacks on those in the top right hand corner. In fact Dawkins might do well to build alliances with those Liberal religious believers in the top left corner (like Keith Ward) with whom he probably has far more in common than he does with *any* of those over to the right (who include atheists like Stalin, of course).

The noise and smoke generated by the battle over religion has tended to obscure a no less significant debate. I believe the really crucial dispute is not between the believers at the top and the atheists at the bottom — it's *between the Liberals on the left and the Authoritarians on the right*. It's to this underlying, more vital dispute that public attention now needs to be drawn. Drawing attention to it is one aim of this book.

Three

Let's take a closer look at how Liberals and Authoritarians differ when it comes to the mechanics of teaching right from wrong.

If a young person ends up with a seriously confused or mistaken set of beliefs – if, for example, they end up with a highly bigoted, racist point of view – the Liberal will no doubt try to show them the error of their ways by rational persuasion, by pointing out to them the perhaps unforeseen consequences of what they've just said, by revealing how their beliefs involve contradictions, and so on. But for those at the Authoritarian end of the Liberal/ Authoritarian scale, rational persuasion is not an option. The problem with rational persuasion is that it involves getting your subjects to apply their own powers of reason – to think independently. And that, of course, is precisely what the Authoritarian wants to avoid.

So how do Authoritarians get people to believe what they're told to believe? There are many methods. Let's start with two of the most brutal.

Murder and Torture

One of the most effective ways of getting people to accept uncritically what you say is to kill them if they don't. The method may be extreme, but it remains fairly popular. As we saw in chapter one, a number of Islamic countries continue to execute any citizen who publicly rejects the Muslim faith. Of course, here in the post-Enlightenment West executing unbelievers is no longer deemed acceptable. But, before we congratulate ourselves on our religious tolerance, let's remember that in some corners of Europe, Enlightenment is a comparatively recent development. The Spanish Inquisition was still murdering those who dared to question the Authority of the Catholic Church as late as the 1820s.[1] Let's also remind ourselves that atheists can be just as murderously Authoritarian. In Stalinist Russia, anyone who dared publicly to question political Authority was likely to face a slow death in the Gulag.

Another brutal 'educational' technique favoured by some Authoritarians is torture. In Orwell's (1954) novel Nineteen Eighty-Four, the central character, Winston, lives in a totalitarian state in which the over-arching Authority figure, Big Brother, seeks to control, not just people's behaviour, but also what they think and feel. Winston rebels, but is finally caught and tortured. His captors make clear that what they ultimately seek to control is not Winston's behaviour, but his thoughts:

> 'And why do you imagine that we bring people to this place?'
> 'To make them confess.'
> 'No, that is not the reason. Try again.'
> 'To punish them.'
> 'No!' exclaimed O'Brien. His voice had changed extraordinarily, and his face had suddenly become both stern and animated. 'No! Not merely to extract your confession, not to punish you. Shall I tell you why we have brought you here? To cure you! To make you sane! Will you understand, Winston, that no one whom we bring to this place ever leaves our hands uncured? We are not interested in those stupid crimes that you have committed. The Party is not interested in the overt act: the thought is all we care about'
> (Orwell 1954: 265).

In Nineteen Eighty-Four, The Party is not just authoritarian with a small 'a'; it is, even more chillingly, brutally Authoritarian with a capital 'A'. Winston is tortured again and again to make him believe whatever Big Brother tells him to believe: even that two plus two equals five. Winston finally succumbs – he ends up quite genuinely loving Big Brother. He ends up believing that if Big Brother says that two plus two equals five, then two and two *does* equal five.

This is merely a fictional illustration. But there are many real examples. Historically, torture has been employed as an 'educational' device by movements as diverse as the Catholic Church and Pol Pot's Khmer Rouge. Again, post-Enlightenment, few Western Authoritarians are willing to go quite this far in getting people to believe what they're told. Today's Authoritarians tend to prefer subtler, gentler methods.

It would be a mistake to caricature all Authoritarians, as I have defined the term, as cruel and merciless monsters. What makes someone an Authoritarian is the emphasis they place on getting individuals, and particularly the young, to defer more-or-less uncritically to Authority rather than think independently. There's no reason why this sort of 'Authoritarian' can't be entirely selfless and sincere. An Authoritarian teacher may have only the very best of intentions towards his or her charges. Nor does an Authoritarian teacher have to be particularly intimidating. The encouragement to defer to Authority may be accompanied by beaming smiles, not knuckle-stinging raps.

Other 'Educational' Methods

Let's take a look at some other, less extreme, educational methods favoured by Authoritarians. Here's a brief overview of nine standard techniques.

1. Punishment

Many Authoritarians consider punishment an acceptable way of moulding, not just a child's behaviour, but also his or her thoughts. It might be physical punishment, for example. I have a friend whose hands were hit hard with a ruler whenever she dared to question what the nuns at her convent school taught her about right and wrong.

If you're Authoritarian, but uncomfortable about using physical punishment to control thought, there remain many other forms of deterrence available: detention, lines, the withdrawal of privileges and so on. In fact, a fairly benign Authoritarian might use nothing more than mild expressions of disappointment. As I say, Authoritarians don't have to be sadistic monsters.

2. Rewards

Rewards are also useful. You could reward those children who exhibit the beliefs you want them to accept. A well-meaning grandmother might deliberately try to shape her grandson's moral attitudes by giving him sweets whenever he expresses the 'right' sort of belief (this sounds pretty benign, until you find out that the kind of attitudes Granny is trying to inculcate in her grandson are deeply racist).

3. Emotive Imagery and Manipulation

It can also help to present followers with iconic images of their Authority. Let every street corner sport a Big-Brother-style portrait of Our Leader. If the Authority is represented surrounded by children, perhaps smiling serenely with golden rays of glory emanating from their head, then so much the better. Those Baghdad murals of Saddam Hussein spring to mind, though of course it is within religious traditions that such iconic images of Authority are most often found. Just like the ubiquitous posters of Big Brother in Orwell's *Nineteen Eight-Four*, religious icons provide useful reminders that, like Big Brother, God is constantly monitoring not just your actions, but your thoughts too.

4. Social Pressure

Social pressure can be used to stigmatize certain questions and beliefs. It can be used to make them seem embarrassing or even shameful. For example, in some communities it's not socially acceptable to admit to having doubts about whether or not God exists.

People would be affronted by a public expression of such questions. Subtle, and maybe not so subtle, psychological pressure would be brought to bear. If you feel it's not the done thing to ask questions or express doubts, you may end up censoring yourself.[2]

Of course, the pressure not to question, discuss openly or consider different points of view can be applied without any explicit admission that this is going on. A colleague recently told me that, as a pupil of a Catholic School back in the late 1960s, she once asked her teacher why Catholics thought contraception was wrong. She wasn't *rejecting* the Catholic view. She was merely asking what the justification for it was. The response was brusque. She was told not to ask such questions and sent to the head teacher, who asked her why she was 'obsessed with sex'. What I found particularly striking about this story is my colleague added that even before she asked the offending question, she knew she shouldn't. No one ever explicitly said, 'Don't question', but that was the message that had nevertheless been subtly communicated by a look here, a frown there, the reverential tone in which certain ideas were communicated, and so on. Even when there's no explicit censorship, an Authoritarian regime can still climb inside your head and shut down those lines of thought or questioning it finds objectionable. Or, more accurately, it can get you to close those lines of thought down yourself. This same colleague tells me that even today, 35 years after her Catholic 'education' was complete, she still feels uncomfortable whenever she finds herself daring to question a Catholic belief.

5. Repetition

Another popular Authoritarian method of moulding young minds is rote learning and mindless repetition. Get people to recite what you want them to believe over and over again. It doesn't matter whether they believe it, or even understand it, to begin with. There's still a good chance belief will eventually take root. Most religions encourage the endless repetition of key words and phrases – 'Hail Mary Mother of God ...', 'Hare Krishna, Hare Rama ...' – particularly when subjects are in a trance-like state (such as prayer) that makes them all the more suggestible.

Mindless repetition seems to work especially well when it's applied in a situation in which the subject feels a powerful social pressure to conform. Totalitarian regimes are fond of lining up pupils in playgrounds for a daily recitation of the regime's key tenets. Here, the child is expected not only to repeat the regime's mantras, but to do so in a situation where any deviation will result in a thousand pairs of eyes immediately turned in their direction. Regimented acts of worship can have the same effect.[3]

6. Control and Censorship

Authoritarians are also generally quick to realize that if you want people to believe what they're told, it's unwise to expose them to alternative systems of belief. Totalitarian states tend to eliminate 'unhealthy' books from libraries if the books contradict the regime. The texts are removed on the grounds that they will only 'confuse' people. Authoritarian religious schools sometimes try to stop their pupils being exposed to atheist and other religious points of view on similar grounds: the presence of these other points of view can only succeed in 'muddling' children.

7. Isolation

Certainly, Authoritarians often consider it unwise to allow their own children to mix with the sons and daughters of unbelievers, from whom they may pick up unacceptable beliefs. In the UK, hermetically sealed-off religious schools are not unusual. Students at Dewsbury's Islamic Tarbiyah Academy are allegedly taught that

> 'the enemies of Allah' have schemed to poison the thinking and minds of [Muslim] youth and to plant the spirit of unsteadiness and moral depravity in their lives. Parents are told that they betray their children if they allow them to befriend non-Muslims (*The Times* 2005: 25).

Most of the West's established religions have operated similarly divisive 'educational' policies in the recent past. Some still do.

8. Uncertainty

Authoritarians also tend to play on our insecurities and the discomfort we feel when faced with uncertainty. Often, they offer a simple set of rules and principles designed to give meaning to and cover every aspect of life. By constantly harping on the vagaries, complexities and meaninglessness of life outside this belief system, the pure, geometric, unshakeable certainties offered by a political or religious Authority can be made to seem increasingly attractive.

9. Tribalism

Another mechanism that can be used to twist our perceptions in an Authority's favour is our tendency towards tribalism. Human beings are peculiarly attracted to them-and-us thinking. By holding up the twisted looking-glass of tribalism, in which 'they' appear dirty, smelly, amoral and perhaps even less than fully human, while 'we' take on a noble countenance (we may even find ourselves reflected back as 'the chosen people' or 'the master race'), an Authority can foster still deeper feelings of loyalty to the group, its leadership and its beliefs, making it still more difficult for its members to question them.

There are, in short, all sorts of ways in which a person's beliefs can be shaped other than by critical reflection and rational persuasion (and these nine examples are certainly not exhaustive). Some of these methods are brutal. Others are comparatively benign. Of course, an Authoritarian need not use any of them. They may simply insist on uncritical acceptance of the judgements of Authority without utilizing any of the techniques described above. However, most established religions still use many of these techniques. Religious schools have traditionally been heavily reliant on many of them. Totalitarian regimes rarely flinch from using the most brutal.

Most Liberals, on the other hand, are instinctively wary of most if not all of these 'educational' devices. Why?

The answer is that they are essentially manipulative. You've no doubt spotted that whether or not the beliefs in question are actually *true* is completely irrelevant so far as the effectiveness of these methods is concerned. They all involve trying to get someone to believe something without providing any grounds for supposing the belief is actually correct. Isolation, censorship and control, uncertainty, mindless repetition, reward, punishment and other kinds of emotional and psychological manipulation – you can use all these techniques to induce the belief that the Earth is round and that Paris is the capital of France. But they may just as easily be applied to induce the beliefs that white people are morally superior to black, that Big Brother loves you, and that there are fairies at the bottom of the garden.

Brainwashing

Incidentally, Taylor (2005: 23), a research scientist in physiology at the University of Oxford who has published a study of brainwashing, recently wrote that five core techniques consistently show up:

> One striking fact about brainwashing is its consistency. Whether the context is a prisoner of war camp, a cult's headquarters or a radical mosque, five core techniques keep cropping up: isolation, control, uncertainty, repetition and emotional manipulation.

Although Taylor doesn't make the connection, what's striking about these five core techniques is that *religious schools have traditionally been very heavily reliant upon them.*

Some will balk at the suggestion that this sort of traditional religious schooling involves brainwashing, or something close to it. But perhaps it's time to call a spade a spade – surely the determined application of these kinds of 'educational' techniques does come uncomfortably near to brainwashing, whether it's carried out by al Qaeda or the Church of England.

The Filter of Reason

At this point, some will be plagued by the following worry: 'But hang on, isn't reason itself just another form of brainwashing? Isn't it just another way of exerting power over young minds? Why is it any better than these other forms of thought-control?'

The answer is that, unlike the techniques of psychological manipulation we've been examining, the attractive thing about appealing to someone's power of reason is that it strongly favours beliefs that are *true*. Cogent argument doesn't easily lend itself to inducing false beliefs. Try, for example, to construct a strong, well-reasoned case capable of withstanding critical scrutiny for believing that the Antarctic is populated by crab-people or that the Earth's core is made of cheese. You're not going to find it easy.

Sound reasoning and critical thought tend to act as a filter on false beliefs. Admittedly, this filter is not one hundred per cent reliable – false beliefs will inevitably get through. But it does tend to allow into a person's mind only those beliefs that have at least a fairly good chance of being correct.

You might think of your mind as a receptacle – a basket towards which all sorts of beliefs are tumbling. There are innumerable beliefs that might end up lodging in your mind, of course, from sensible ones such as the Earth is round to ridiculous ones such as the Antarctic is populated by crab-people. Your powers of reason act as a filter. Use reason to filter incoming beliefs and you are far less likely to end up with a head full of nonsense.

Those Authoritarians who apply psychological manipulation try, in effect, to *bypass this filter*. They attempt to inject beliefs into the child's mind directly, without engaging the child's rational, critical faculties. Often, the Authoritarian will be quite explicit that the child should *turn their filter off*. That's precisely what is being suggested when the child is instructed to accept uncritically what they are told as a matter of 'faith'. Encouraging faith in the pronouncements of an Authority – be it Big Brother or a religious leader – is one of the Authoritarian's favourite educational techniques. Within an Authoritarian regime, those who show a wholly blind and trusting faith in Authority are often considered *especially* virtuous. The ease with which they can be manipulated by Authority is a badge the faithful wear with pride.

Unlike the manipulative techniques we've been examining, reason is a double-edged sword. It cuts both ways. It doesn't automatically favour the teacher's beliefs over the pupil's. It favours the truth, and so places the teacher and the pupil on a level playing field. If, as a teacher, you try to use reason to persuade, you may discover that your pupil can show that it is actually *you*, not them, that's mistaken. That's a risk many moral 'educators' are not prepared to take.

The 'Modern Parents'

Historically, these manipulative methods of moulding young minds are most closely associated with established religion and totalitarian states. However, even the most politically correct of parents may find themselves drifting into using them.

John Fardell writes a cartoon strip called 'The Modern Parents', in which two ridiculously right-on, muesli-eating, tree-hugging parents – Malcolm and Cressida – attempt morally to educate their two sons Tarquin and Guinevere. One reason I find this cartoon strip amusing is that, despite their impeccable 'politically correct' credentials, Malcolm and Cressida can't rationally back up what they believe. As a result, they inevitably end up falling back on psychological manipulation. They use emotional blackmail, reward and punishment, social pressure and all sorts of other tricks to get their two sons to embrace the same views as themselves.

© John Fardell

The moral is that psychological manipulation as an 'educational' device is something we can all very easily slip into relying on, whatever our beliefs and no matter how 'liberal' we might think we are.

Striking a Balance

Liberals generally try to steer clear of the kind of manipulative techniques I've been describing. But of course few would suggest we can get rid of them altogether. After all, Liberals are not against rules and discipline when it comes to controlling behaviour. And by showing our disapproval of and punishing certain kinds of behaviour, we're bound to end up shaping the child's moral beliefs too. There are all sorts of ways in which we inevitably mould children's attitudes other than by giving them good reasons and justifications.

The issue is one of balance. Liberals can admit that we unavoidably end up shaping children's moral beliefs by these means, whether we mean to or not. The Liberal may even admit that this is, to some limited extent, desirable. They merely insist that *we should nevertheless make sure that children are raised to think carefully, critically and for themselves about moral issues*. It's this that sets the Liberal apart from the Authoritarian, who places greater emphasis on deference to Authority.

Again, if you're a teacher or parent you might ask yourself just how Liberal or Authoritarian you tend to be in the way you morally educate your charges. Perhaps, while you do sometimes resort to psychological manipulation (and, to some extent, we all do), you also think it's important that the young citizens in your care are helped and encouraged to develop into autonomous individuals capable of thinking for themselves. If so, that makes your attitude more-Liberal-than-Authoritarian. That, I would argue, is what it should be.

The Positive Side to Liberal Education

Let's now look in more detail at the Liberal alternative to Authority-based moral and religious education.

One way of being Liberal-with-a-capital-L would of course be to ignore morality altogether, to abandon each child to invent his or her own morality from scratch, within a moral vacuum. That's not the method advocated here. This book recommends a much more specific sort of approach, an approach that involves a training in and the fostering of what might broadly be termed 'thinking skills and virtues'. Children should be encouraged to scrutinize their own beliefs and explore other points of view. While not wanting to be overly prescriptive, I would suggest that skills to be cultivated should at least include the ability to:

- reveal and question underlying assumptions,
- figure out the perhaps unforeseen consequences of a moral decision or point of view,
- spot and diagnose faulty reasoning,
- weigh up evidence fairly and impartially,
- make a point clearly and concisely,
- take turns in a debate, and listen attentively without interrupting,
- argue without personalizing a dispute,
- look at issues from the point of view of others, and
- question the appropriateness of, or the appropriateness of acting on, one's own feelings.

Acquiring these skills involves developing, not just a level of intellectual maturity, but a fair degree of emotional maturity too. For example, turn-taking requires patience and self-control. Judging impartially involves identifying and taking account of your own emotional biases. By thinking critically and carefully about your own beliefs and attitudes, you may develop insights into your own character. By stepping outside of your own viewpoint and looking at issues from the stance of another, you can develop a greater empathy with and understanding of others. So by engaging in this kind of philosophical, critical activity, you are likely to develop not only the ability to reason cogently, but also what now tends to be called 'emotional intelligence' (which is why the Director of Antidote – a British organization that works with schools to help develop emotional literacy – recently endorsed this kind of philosophical activity as an effective tool in aiding emotional development).[4] Although I have emphasized the importance of reason, I don't wish to downplay the importance of emotional development. They are deeply intertwined.

Notice that many of these skills can only be developed, or at least are most effectively developed, by engaging in group activities, by getting children collectively to discuss and debate issues *together*. These are skills and virtues that are best taught and mastered, not in isolation, but through interaction within a 'community of inquiry'. For that reason, many philosophy for children's programmes are based around structured, open-ended group discussion. So the kind of Liberal approach recommended here certainly acknowledges the importance of a shared, social dimension to moral education. It's not about severing all social ties and abandoning each individual child to 'think up' their own morality within their own hermetically sealed-off universe. Quite the reverse. Exploring issues together may help foster interpersonal skills and a sense of community and belonging.[5]

The approach described above might loosely be termed 'philosophical', though I should stress that doesn't mean children should be given an academic course on the history of philosophy. What it means is that they should be trained and encouraged to approach questions in a particular kind of way. We should get them into the habit of thinking in an open, reflective, critical way, so that these intellectual, emotional and social skills and virtues are developed.[6]

Clearly, *the sort of philosophical approach to moral education recommended here is anti-Authoritarian.* Those who favour Authority-based moral and religious education will reject it. Encouraging pupils to think for themselves, to debate freely and openly different moral and religious points of view, is precisely what those who think children should be taught to defer more or less uncritically to Authority on moral and religious matters are against.[7]

Can Children be Philosophical?

Of course, all this presupposes that thinking philosophically is something children *can* do. But can they?

There's good empirical evidence that they can. There have been a number of studies and programmes involving philosophy with children in several countries. The results are impressive.

One notable example is the Buranda State School, a small Australian primary school near Brisbane, which in 1997 introduced into all its classes a philosophy programme along much the lines outlined above. Children collectively engaged in structured debates addressing philosophical questions that they themselves had come up with, following a *Philosophy in Schools* programme using materials developed by the philosopher Philip Cam and others. The effects were dramatic. The school showed marked academic improvement across the curriculum. A report on the success of the programme says,

> [f]or the last four years, students at Buranda have achieved outstanding academic results. This had not been the case prior to the teaching of Philosophy. In the systemic Year 3/5/7 tests (previously Yr 6 Test), our students performed below the state mean in most areas in 1996. Following the introduction of Philosophy in 1997, the results of our students improved significantly and have been maintained or improved upon since that time (Buranda State School Showcase 2003 Submission Form).

There were substantial payoffs in terms of behaviour too. The report indicates 'significantly improved outcomes' occurred in the social behaviour of the students:

> The respect for others and the increase in individual self esteem generated in the community of inquiry have permeated all aspects of school life. We now have few behaviour problems at our school (and we do have some difficult students). Students are less impatient with each other, they are more willing to accept their own mistakes as a normal part of learning and they discuss problems as they occur. As one Yr 5 child said, 'Philosophy is a good example of how you should behave in the playground with your friends' ... Bullying behaviour is rare at Buranda, with there being no reported incidence of bullying this year to date. A visiting academic commented, 'Your children don't fight, they negotiate' ... Visitors to the school are constantly making reference to the 'feel'

or 'spirit' of the place. We believe it's the way our children treat each other. The respect for others generated in the community of inquiry has permeated all aspects of school life (Buranda State School Showcase 2003 Submission Form).

Of course this is a single example – hardly conclusive evidence by itself. But it's not the only example. In 2001–2002, Professor Keith Topping, a senior psychologist, in conjunction with the University of Dundee, studied the effects on introducing one hour per week of philosophy (using a *Thinking Through Philosophy* programme developed by Paul Cleghorn) at a number of upper primary schools in Clackmannanshire, including schools in deprived areas. Teachers were given two days of training. The study involved a whole range of tests, and also a control group of schools with no philosophy programme. The children involved were aged 11–12. This study found that after one year,

- The incidence of children supporting opinion with evidence doubled, but 'control' classes remained unchanged;
- There was evidence that children's self-esteem and confidence rose markedly;
- The incidence of teachers asking open-ended questions (to better develop enquiry) doubled;
- There was evidence that class ethos and discipline improved noticeably;
- The ratio of teacher/pupil talk halved for teachers and doubled for pupils. Controls remained the same; and
- All classes improved significantly (statistically) in verbal, non-verbal and quantitative reasoning. No control class changed. This means children were more intelligent (av. 6.5 IQ points) after one year on the programme.

These benefits were retained. When the children were tested again at 14, after two years at secondary school *without* a philosophy programme, their CAT scores were exactly the same (that's to say, the improvements that had previously been gained were retained), while the control group scores actually went *down* during those two years. Three secondary schools were involved and the results replicated themselves over each school.[8] Again, this is only one study. No doubt such results should be treated with caution. But, they do lend considerable weight to the claim that not only *can* children of this age think philosophically, it's also highly beneficial. A recent study strongly supports the view that philosophy for children provides measurable educational benefits for children even in their first year of school.[9]

To sum up: there's good evidence that children, even fairly young children, *can* think philosophically.[10] And, while more research needs to be done, there's a growing body of evidence that it's good for them academically, socially and emotionally.[11] The kinds of skills such philosophy programmes foster are, surely, just the sort of skills we need new citizens to develop. Or so I'll now argue.

Four

We've already seen that the kind of Liberal approach to moral and religious education outlined in the previous chapter can deliver important educational benefits. Let's now further develop the case for embracing a Liberal approach.

One advantage of a little training in and experience of critical thinking and rational debate is that it can help provide a lifetime's immunization against the wiles of second-hand car salesmen, astrologers, feng-shui consultants, get-rich-quick pyramid-scheme sellers, Holocaust deniers and other purveyors of snake oil. The ability to spot when someone has committed a logical howler, attempted to psychologically manipulate you or otherwise tried to pull the wool over your eyes is always useful no matter what your walk in life.

In this chapter, we'll see why it's also important for a healthy democracy that citizens possess these skills.

Democracy and the Liberal Approach

Democracy and freedom of thought and expression are usually thought to go hand in hand. Certainly there's a powerful case for saying that any healthy democracy requires freedom of thought and expression. Candidates need to be free to say what they stand for, and criticize their opponents. Citizens need to be able to say what they want, and why they want it. They too must be free to criticize the views of the Government, and of others, and explain why they believe their opponents are wrong. Without this kind of free exchange of arguments and ideas, democracy is a farce.

Even in a country that is 'free', and not at all Authoritarian with a capital 'A' (certainly, no one ever tells its citizens, 'This is what you must believe, *because I say so*'), the kinds of psychological manipulation and pressure outlined in chapter three might still be applied to sway the mind of a population that had never been much trained or indeed encouraged to think carefully and critically about moral and political issues. These various manipulative mechanisms can combine to form an instrument upon which a skilled and charismatic leader can play a highly seductive melody, a melody to which those whose critical defences are weak will find hard not to march. It's upon such instruments that the world's most dangerous pied pipers play their tunes.

For example, a daily diet of iconic imagery, them-and-us thinking, peer pressure, social stigma and sensationalized and terrifying news reportage might be used to manipulate citizens whose critical defences and capacity for autonomous critical reflection are pretty weak. Clearly, that would be a dangerous situation. Here we would have a public, ostensibly free to think, say and do much as they please, living within a democracy, comprised of individuals who are nevertheless largely the puppets of those controlling the mechanisms by which the psychological manipulation was applied. These citizens might be 'freedom loving people', but the ease with which their strings could be pulled would mean their freedom was of a rather limited sort.

Some cynics might claim this is already the situation in at least one democracy, where jingoistic news channels, shock jocks and Christian fundamentalists pull the strings of a population transfixed by the images of crime and terrorism that slide perpetually across their TV screens.[1] Whether or not that is the situation, there's surely a good case for saying that a healthy democracy needs citizens capable of autonomous critical reflection – it needs individuals who are 'Enlightened' in Kant's sense of the word. Leaving a sound

Liberal education out of the democratic mix leaves citizens highly vulnerable to psychological manipulation.

The 'Marketplace of Ideas'

Probably the best-known arguments for freedom of thought and expression are to be found in Mill's (1991) *On Liberty*. Mill offers four arguments for freedom of thought and expression, one of which is as follows.

History can supply many examples where an Authority, absolutely confident in the correctness of its own view, has attempted to gag those who, it has subsequently turned out, were actually correct. That was the case when the Inquisition attempted to silence Galileo. It was the Church that was mistaken, not Galileo. The strength of the conviction of those in Authority provides neither them nor us with any guarantee that they are right. Human beings, no matter how wise, make mistakes. And the only way in which those mistakes will be corrected is if we are prepared to expose our beliefs to criticism. Mill argues that no one has any right to feel certain about a belief if those most motivated and best qualified to subject it to critical scrutiny have been gagged. If an Authority silences all criticism of their own judgements, then not only do they have little warrant for their own feeling of certainty, *we shouldn't have much confidence in their judgement either.*[2]

Mill, in effect, suggests that society should operate a *marketplace of ideas*. All ideas and arguments may enter the market. Mill believes that the ideas most likely to survive in the open competition of this market will be those that are true. A sort of Darwinian selection takes place: false ideas and theories are weeded out by close critical scrutiny. Only those beliefs that are true (or probably true) are likely to survive.

Now a standard criticism of the suggestion that we operate a free and open marketplace of ideas is that *what makes an idea flourish in the marketplace is not necessarily its truth*. Human beings are not perfectly rational. We are impressed by many factors, often by packaging as much as by content. We are easily swayed by the various kinds of psychological manipulation outlined in chapter three. Ideas may flourish not because they are rationally superior, but because they are disseminated by those with access to far more powerful mechanisms to get their ideas across. Take the advertising industry, for example. It exists, not to help those beliefs that are true rise to the top, but to propagate those ideas that best help its clients. It's very effective. Given all this, some might say we really can't afford to operate an entirely free and open market of ideas. That will only make us easy prey to those best placed psychologically to manipulate us.

Still, even if Mill was over-optimistic about the ability of human beings not to be swayed by these other factors, if we are going to have any sort of marketplace of ideas – as surely any democracy must – isn't there a strong case for saying that individuals need to be encouraged and trained to think carefully and critically, so they are not so easily seduced by the psychological manipulators? Isn't that our best chance of getting at the truth?

Human beings are never going to be perfect truth-detectors, but surely, in a democracy, we all need to be as good as we can be.

Milgram's Experiment

Here's another reason why raising Enlightened citizens might be a good idea.

Humans have a disastrously strong in-built tendency to defer to authority. This was demonstrated particularly vividly by the psychologist Stanley Milgram back in the 1950s. Struck by the way in which concentration camp guards in Nazi Germany attempted to excuse themselves by insisting they were 'only obeying orders', Milgram set out to show that the same could never happen in the US. He designed an experiment to establish what strength of electric shock an ordinary American citizen would administer to a stranger if asked to do so by a white-coated authority figure.

Subjects were recruited through a newspaper advertisement to take part in a 'study of memory' for which they would receive a small payment. Each participant was paired with a stooge who pretended to be another member of the public. The participant was told that one of them would be arbitrarily selected as the 'learner' and the other as the 'teacher'. In fact the actor always became the 'learner'. After seeing their pupil strapped into an electric chair, the 'teacher' was taken to a neighbouring room where they could speak to their pupil via an intercom. They were asked to teach and test their partner. When the 'learner' made a mistake, the participant was told to administer an electric shock. The shocks were delivered from a board of 30 lever switches that ranged from 15 volts up to 400 volts. The board was also labelled descriptively, from 'slight shock' up to 'Danger: severe shock'. When a shock was administered, a buzzer sounded, a needle on a voltage meter deflected and lights flashed. The shocks the subject was asked to give were mild at first, but gradually escalated in intensity. As the voltage increased, the actor next door feigned increasing levels of discomfort and alarm. He would beg to be released.

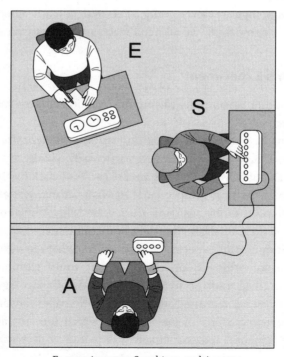

E: experimenter; S: subject; and A: actor.

At 300 volts he would kick the wall. At the next level, marked 'extreme intensity shock', he became silent (as if dead or unconscious).

Milgram wanted to see how far up the scale Joe Public would be prepared to go if ordered to do so by an 'authority figure' dressed in a white coat. Just what level of shock would an average US citizen be prepared to deliver before they refused to continue with the experiment?

The results were extraordinary. Milgram found that sixty-five per cent of his subjects went right to the end of the scale, beyond the point where the participants believed they had killed their 'learner'. It appears that around sixty-five per cent of ordinary American citizens will electrocute another human being to death if told to do so by a white-coated authority-figure.

True, many participants became agitated and concerned about the fate of their subject. When they expressed their concerns, the authority figure would respond by saying 'Please continue', 'The experiment requires that you continue', 'It is absolutely essential that you continue' and 'You have no other choice – you must go on'. But no threats were issued. And yet, astonishingly, despite feeling that what they were doing was very wrong, the participants found the pressure to defer to the authority-figure overwhelming. In fact, not only did the majority proceed to murder the 'learner', not one of them stopped before reaching 300 volts – the point at which the 'learner' began to kick the wall.

It turns out that the soldiers who ran Auschwitz and who said they were 'only obeying orders' weren't weird, inhuman monsters. They were just like the rest of us. And remember that the soldiers at Auschwitz had the excuse that, had they disobeyed orders, they might themselves have been punished or killed. No such threats were made to Milgram's subjects.

Of course, most of us don't believe we would electrocute another human being to death if instructed to do so by an authority figure. We believe that in such circumstances *we* would act differently. We believe *we* would stand up and denounce the whole procedure as monstrous. Unfortunately, there's good evidence that we flatter ourselves. It seems that, in similar circumstances, most of us will follow the instructions of authority to the bitter end.

Glover's and the Oliners' Research

What Milgram demonstrated, in effect, is the extent to which we're all *moral sheep*. We tend naturally to lack the inner resources to identify and stand up for what is right when pitted against a malign authority. We tend to go with the flow, follow the flock, do, and even believe, what we're told to by those we perceive to be in positions of 'authority' over us.[3]

So how do we avoid raising moral sheep? Professor Jonathan Glover, Director of the Centre for Medical Law and Ethics at King's College, London, has conducted research into the backgrounds of both those who were most eager to join in killing in places like Nazi Germany, Rwanda and Bosnia, and also those who worked to save lives, often at great risk to themselves. As Glover (1999) explained in an interview in *The Guardian*,

> If you look at the people who shelter Jews under the Nazis, you find a number of things about them. One is that they tended to have a different kind of upbringing from the average person, they tended to be brought up in a non-authoritarian way, brought up to have sympathy with other people and to discuss things rather than just do what they were told.

Glover adds, 'I think that teaching people to think rationally and critically actually can make a difference to people's susceptibility to false ideologies.'

Oliner and Oliner (1992) conducted an extensive and detailed study into the backgrounds of both those who went along with the Final Solution and those who rescued victims. In *The Altruistic Personality—Rescuers of Jews in Nazi Europe*, they report that the most dramatic difference between the parents of those who rescued and those who did not lay in the extent to which parents placed greater emphasis on explaining, rather than on punishment and discipline.

> [P]arents of rescuers depended significantly less on physical punishment and significantly more on reasoning (p. 179).

> [I]t is in their reliance on reasoning, explanations, suggestions of ways to remedy harm done, persuasion, and advice that the parents of rescuers differed from non-rescuers (p. 181).

Oliner and Oliner add that 'reasoning communicates a message of respect for and trust in children that allows them to feel a sense of personal efficacy and warmth toward others'. By contrast, the non-rescuers tended to feel 'mere pawns, subject to the power of external authorities' (p. 177). Incidentally, Oliner and Oliner (1992: 156) found that while religious belief was also a factor, 'religiosity was only weakly related to rescue'.

If Glover's and the Oliners' findings and conclusions are correct, then they mesh with Milgram's. Given that human beings have a disastrous tendency to defer to Authority anyway, surely the last thing we should do is reinforce this tendency. If we seek to produce truly moral individuals, and not just a moral sheep, we should not, as those at the Authoritarian end of the Liberal/Authoritarian scale want, seek to strip away from individuals the responsibility to establish what is right and what is wrong. Rather, we should confront them with that responsibility. We should also equip them with the skills they will need to discharge that responsibility properly.

Of course, there can be advantages to a society within which a powerful moral Authority is at work. If a strict moral code is drilled into all individuals from a very young age, perhaps backed up with threats of divine retribution should they err, and if the questioning of moral Authority is not tolerated, then perhaps a society will emerge in which crime hardly exists and the streets are litter free. You may ask what is wrong with that.

Well, let's hope that this Authority remains fairly benign. What is terrifying about such societies is what their members might do if so commanded. Once their confidence in their own ability to distinguish right from wrong has been eroded, individuals can be led into committing all sorts of horrors. The Twentieth Century has shown this to be no idle worry. Just as Milgram initially thought that what happened in Germany could never happen in the US, so we all have a rather complacent tendency to suppose 'it could never happen here'. As I say, the evidence suggests otherwise.

Of course, even someone raised in the Liberal way recommended here may end up committing some unspeakable atrocity. Perhaps some have. The preceding argument is not that those raised within a Liberal regime – the kind of regime you find at a school like Liberalia High – will *never* commit such atrocities. It's that human beings have a demonstrable and clearly dangerous tendency to behave like moral sheep, and that a Liberal approach would seem to be our best defence against this tendency. This gives us a powerful reason for favouring the Liberal approach, a reason not easily outweighed by other factors.

There's a further, related reason for favouring a Liberal approach. No doubt the risk of atrocities will always exist, but at least those raised in a Liberal way can be reasoned with. They will feel themselves obliged to consider alternative points of view and to take seriously our criticisms. We can still reach them. The more they have been raised to defer to Authority, on the other hand, the harder it will be to get through to them. Those raised to defer blindly to an Authority might as well have cotton wool in their ears so far as our arguments and objections are concerned.

Muslim Terrorists

The dangers of failing to raise new citizens to think critically and independently – and the perils of getting them to defer uncritically to religious Authority instead – have recently been brought home by the rise of Britain's homegrown Muslim terrorists.

The writer Hanif Kureishi has explained how, to find out more about the faith of his father, he spent the early 1990s touring various London mosques. What he found disturbed him. He met many young men who, he said, while they seemed far too 'weedy and polite' to want to kill anyone, talked ominously of 'going to train' abroad.

These men believed they had access to the truth, as stated in the Qu'ran. There could be no doubt – or even much dispute about social, moral and political problems – because God had the answers. Therefore, for them, to argue with the Truth was like trying to disagree with the facts of geometry. For them the source of all virtue and vice was the pleasure and displeasure of Allah. To be a responsible human being was to submit to this. As the Muslim writer Shabbir Akhtar put it in his book, *A Faith for all Seasons*, 'Allah is the subject of faith' and loving obedience, not of rational inquiry or purely discursive thought. Unaided human reason is inferior in status to the gift of faith. Indeed, reason is useful only in so far as it finds a use in the larger service of faith (*The Guardian* 2005).

Kureishi is not the only Muslim to believe that 'too many Muslims are incapable of establishing a critical culture that goes beyond a stifling Islamic paradigm' (*The Guardian* 2005). The Muslim academic Tariq Ramadan says, 'Muslims now need, more than ever, to be self-critical. That means educating young Muslims in more than religious formalism' (*The Guardian* 2005). Kureishi believes that this emphasis on unquestioning obedience and faith, and the absence of any encouragement or training in thinking freely and critically, is one of the root causes of violent Islamic fundamentalism in the UK.

While a failure to encourage critical and independent thought, particularly about one's own religion, is clearly not the *whole* cause of the recent terrorist attacks, it's plausible that it has at least been a contributory factor.[4] Radical Muslim clerics can be skilled in applying the kinds of psychological manipulation outlined in chapter three to cast a hypnotic spell over those whom they've been charged with educating. One of the most effective defences against this potentially highly dangerous form of manipulation is to make sure that every new citizen has received at least some exposure to the kind of philosophical training outlined in chapter three.

Tony Blair wants Britain to have more 'faith schools'. But he is not particularly clear what sort of faith schools he has in mind. This is a crucial omission. By all means let's allow faith schools (though whether the State should pay for them is another matter). But not the kind of faith schools that insist on deference to

Authority, that rely heavily on psychological manipulation, and that strongly discourage independent critical thought. Such schools provide the perfect fodder for religious zealots to transform into weapons of jihad.

Dawkins (2001) once said that 'To fill a world with religion, or religions of the Abrahamic kind, is like littering the streets with loaded guns'. That may not be true of all religion. But it is, I would suggest, closer to the truth when it comes to *Authoritarian* religion. It's probably fairly accurate when it comes to highly Authoritarian religious schools.

Blaming the Holocaust on Atheism and the Enlightenment

We've seen that Glover's research led him to the conclusion that the best way to avoid moral catastrophes like those we have seen in Nazi Germany and Russia is to raise people to have sympathy with others, and to think critically and independently rather than defer to Authority. A Liberal approach to moral education, suggests Glover, would seem to be our best defence against such calamities.

But not everyone would agree with that. Some argue that actually, *a Liberal approach is just as likely, perhaps more likely, to result in moral catastrophe.* It's even suggested there's historical evidence to support that claim. The Holocaust is often mentioned in this regard.

Take the British journalist and social commentator Phillips. As we saw in chapter one, Phillips blames many of our current social ills on the Enlightenment. She also thinks the Enlightenment was responsible for the Holocaust.

> The Enlightenment gave us freedom and liberal values; but it also gave us ... the Holocaust (Phillips 1998: 189).

Phillips doesn't spell out exactly how the Enlightenment gave us the Holocaust. Perhaps that's because she thinks it's obvious. Let's try joining the dots ourselves. How might the Enlightenment and the Holocaust be linked?

Some find the connection in atheism. 'The Enlightenment gave us atheism', they say, with some justification; '... and two of the greatest orgies of killing the world has ever known were conducted during the Twentieth Century by atheist regimes: Nazi Germany and Stalinist Russia. So you see, this shows that you atheists are just as bad if not worse than we believers. And it establishes that the Enlightenment is the root cause of these atrocities.'

But is atheism to blame? It's often claimed that Hitler was an atheist. Take the US journalist Ann Coulter, for example. In her bestselling *How to Talk to a Liberal — If You Must*, Coulter (2004) says that Hitler was an atheist who denounced Christianity. Indeed, Coulter (2004: 165) claims that 'all the great mass murders of the last century ... were atheists'.

Actually, Hitler was raised as, and repeatedly claimed to be, a Christian. Hitler even used *The Bible* to justify his persecution of the Jews. Here's an example:

> My feelings as a Christian point me to my Lord and Savior
> as a fighter. It points me to the man who once in loneliness,
> surrounded by a few followers, recognized these Jews for
> what they were and summoned men to fight against them and
> who, God's truth! was greatest not as a sufferer but as a fighter.
> In boundless love as a Christian and as a man I read through
> the passage which tells us how the Lord at last rose in His might
> and seized the scourge to drive out of the Temple the brood of
> vipers and adders. How terrific was His fight for the world
> against the Jewish poison. Today, after two thousand years,
> with deepest emotion I recognize more profoundly than ever
> before the fact that it was for this that He had to shed His
> blood upon the Cross. As a Christian I have no duty to allow
> myself to be cheated, but I have the duty to be a fighter for truth
> and justice ... And if there is anything which could demonstrate
> that we are acting rightly it is the distress that daily grows.
> For as a Christian I have also a duty to my own people
> (Adolf Hitler, in a speech on 12 April 1922, from Baynes
> 1942: 19–20).

That doesn't sound like an atheist talking. Hitler targeted the 'godless'. His soldiers wore belt buckles saying 'Got mit uns' – God with us. Hitler even refused to tolerate secular schools because he thought moral instruction must be grounded in religious faith:

> Secular schools can never be tolerated because such a school has no religious instruction and a general moral instruction without a religious foundation is built on air; consequently, all character training and religion must be derived from faith (Helmreich 1979: 241).

What is true is that later Hitler did increasingly turn against Christianity, which he saw as a potential threat to his own power. In fact Hitler ended up calling Christianity 'an invention of sick brains' (Burleigh 2001: 718). But even when Hitler began to turn against Christianity, *he continued to detest atheism:*

> We don't want to educate anyone in atheism
> (Trevor-Roper 1988: 6).

> An uneducated man, on the other hand, runs the risk of going over to atheism (which is a return to the state of the animal)...
> (Trevor-Roper 1988: 59)

Coulter focuses exclusively on Hitler's later attacks on Christianity, entirely overlooking his earlier enthusiasm for Christianity, the partly Christian roots of his own anti-Semitism, and his ongoing abhorence of atheism.

That Hitler was an atheist is one of those 'factoids' that those keen to discredit atheism often repeat. But, while many might like it to be true, the evidence doesn't support it.

Stalin, on the other hand, was clearly an atheist. But remember that even if atheism was the root cause of the Gulag (a very dubious claim), and perhaps even the Holocaust (still more dubious), *Liberals don't have to be atheists.* This book does not present an argument for atheism. It presents an argument for a Liberal approach to moral and religious education, an approach that is consistent with both religious belief and a religious upbringing. So if you don't like atheism – fine. You may even believe, if you like, that atheism is responsible for the Gulag. That doesn't yet give you a reason to reject the Liberal approach.

In fact you still have very good reason to be Liberal. Notice that Hitler and Stalin were both highly Authoritarian. Again, let's focus on Hitler for a moment. Even before they came to power, the Nazis were fond of organizing book-burnings of 'unGerman' literature (including the works of Karl Marx). Once he came to power, Hitler ended democracy, banned other political parties, and had political opponents murdered. Hitler suppressed completely the freedom of the press. Journalists and others critical of Hitler and the Nazis risked prison or execution. Josef Goebbels' Ministry of Propaganda was created to control all art, theatre, music, radio and the press – to ensure that only ideas and ideals sanctioned by the Nazis were ever publicly expressed. Hitler and the Nazis were brutally Authoritarian with a capital 'A'.

Stalin, of course, was no more tolerant of criticism. Nor were Mao and Pol Pot. Pol Pot wanted to eradicate not just the reality but even the memory of the old Capitalist Society, so he began by shifting the urban population to the country, away from books, newspapers, films and television. Then he began to 're-educate' them. Those who had been trained to think were most likely to be targeted. At least 1.5 million died.[5]

Mao's 'Cultural Revolution' similarly involved the merciless eradication of all traces of unacceptable culture, which, unfortunately for them, was rooted in the heads of his citizens. Again, Mao focused on the educated, and particularly on educators. The result was the biggest killing spree in history.[6]

What all three of these atheist mass-murderers – Stalin, Mao and Pol Pot – have in common with the mass-murderers of the Holy Inquisition is an obsession with *controlling thought*. In all three cases, we find Authoritarian regimes slaughtering their own citizens *largely because of the thoughts it was suspected those citizens harboured in their heads.* It was, above all, those who were, or were suspected of being, Enlightened, in Kant's sense of the term – those who dared to think and question Authority – who were exterminated like pests. The Twentieth Century saw not only a Jewish Holocaust, but a holocaust of the Enlightened.

Hitler, Stalin, Mao and Pol Pot are all cruelly Authoritarian figures. All are profoundly anti-Liberal. Despite the numerous attempts (from Phillips and countless others) that have been made to blame these atrocities on the Enlightenment and the Liberal ideas to which it gave birth, it is, shall we say, far from obvious that that is where the blame truly lies (though see Appendix One for other suggestions as to how the Enlightenment and the Holocaust might yet be linked).

From the Holy Inquisition to Auschwitz to the Gulag to Mao's Cultural Revolution to Cambodia's Killing Fields, the state-sponsored mass-murder of their own citizens is a speciality of Authoritarian societies, not Liberal ones. If we want to avoid such catastrophes in the future, we should realize that religion, or the lack of it, is largely a red herring. An Authoritarian obsession with thought-control is not.

Conclusion

Many have tried to blame Enlightenment for the moral catastrophes of the Twentieth Century. It's often claimed that the best way to avoid such disasters in the future is to make sure we defer to an external religious Authority that can keep us morally on an even keel and prevent us then sliding into barbarism.

But, ironically, by encouraging greater deference to some external moral Authority it seems we actually *increase* the risk of carnage. It appears our best defence against such atrocities is to raise Enlightened citizens – citizens who are not afraid to think critically and independently about moral, religious and other issues (these being, of course, the very citizens that Stalin, Mao and Pol Pot were most keen to exterminate). If we want to prevent our own society drifting in the same dangerous direction, we need to make sure it remains vigorously Liberal. That means *resisting* moves to encourage young citizens to be more deferential towards external moral Authority – be it a religious Authority or otherwise.

Five

This chapter provides a further argument for Liberalism: not only is it imprudent to hand over responsibility for making moral judgements to some external moral Authority, it *can't* be handed over. The responsibility for making moral judgements has a boomerang-like quality – it always comes back to you.

The chapter concludes by looking at a charge often made against Liberals – that of inconsistency.

When it's Sensible to Trust an Authority

Deferring to authority isn't *always* a bad idea. We do it all the time. No doubt you go to a doctor for a medical opinion, to a plumber for expertise on central heating, to a lawyer for legal advice, and so on. It's pretty reasonable to take the authority's word for it in these cases.

In fact, modern life demands that we trust the expertise of others. The world is now so complex that any one of us can only properly understand how a tiny bit of it works. We can't all be experts on plumbing, science, the law, car mechanics, psychology, and so on. We have to seek out others upon whose expertise we inevitably have to rely.

So what if you go to an authority on some matter, and they give you bad advice? Who's to blame, then, if things then go awry? Suppose, for example, that a student new to chemistry wants to know whether it's safe to dispose of a large lump of potassium by flushing it down the sink. She asks their chemistry professor, who tells them it will be perfectly safe. So the student drops the potassium in the sink. There's a huge explosion that kills another student. Is the student who was given the wrong advice to blame? Can she excuse herself by pointing out that her authority told her to do it?

Yes she can. It was entirely reasonable for the student to trust the advice of her chemistry professor. She had every reason to accept the professor's advice. Generally speaking, if we go to the acknowledged experts for advice, and those experts assure us that something is a good idea when in fact it's a very bad idea, we're not morally culpable when things go wrong as a result.

Why Moral Authorities are Different

But if it's sensible to trust the word of medical, legal and plumbing experts – if we are justified in simply taking their word for it – then why not the word of moral experts?

Suppose someone wants to know what sort of attitude she should have towards those who don't share the same religion as her. She goes to her community's religious and moral Authority for the answer, the Authority to which she has always deferred in the past. Suppose this Authority tells her that it is her moral duty to kill those who don't share the same religious beliefs as her. In fact, suppose this Authority tells her to go out, wire herself to some explosives, wander into a supermarket full of unbelievers, and blow herself up. She takes her moral Authority's word for it (as she always has) and goes out and kills several hundred people. Is this person also blameless?

Intuitively not. Someone who goes out and kills on the instruction of a religious or some other moral Authority does not thereby avoid moral responsibility for what they have done. 'I was only following the instructions of my expert' is not an excuse.

Of course, in the case of the suicide bomber, there may be mitigating factors that make her less blameworthy. For example, if we feel this woman did not really make a free decision – if we suspect she was heavily psychologically manipulated, or perhaps even brainwashed – then we might be more forgiving. But the point remains that she can't absolve herself of responsibility simply by saying 'My moral expert told me it was okay' in the same way that the chemistry student can absolve herself of responsibility by saying 'My chemistry expert told me it was okay'.

Here's one reason why. Notice that the judgement whether someone is expert in a technical area like chemistry, plumbing or car maintenance needn't itself be a technical judgement. You don't need to be an expert on chemistry yourself in order to have good grounds for thinking someone else is a chemistry expert whose advice can safely be followed. But the judgement whether someone is a moral expert whose advice ought in this case to be followed is itself a moral judgement. So you inevitably have to engage your own moral judgement – rely on your own moral compass – in judging whether or not to follow that advice.[1] But then the responsibility for making a significant moral judgement cannot be wholly, or even largely, sloughed off onto an 'expert' in the way that the responsibility for making a judgement about chemistry or car maintenance can.

Taking Advice from Moral Experts and Authorities

None of this is to say that we shouldn't seek moral advice, particularly when it comes to complex moral dilemmas. The advice we receive might be valuable. It might lead us to recognize that we were mistaken in holding a particular moral belief. No doubt some people really are better judges of what's right and what's wrong than are the rest of us. They're 'moral experts' in that sense. Arguably, these moral experts include some priests, imams and rabbis. If so, we might learn by listening to them. They may, in this sense, be 'authoritative'.

However, to accept that some people may be 'authorities' in this sense is not to say that we should more-or-less uncritically defer to them on moral matters. Let's acknowledge that some people may be moral 'authorities' in the sense that they may know more, morally speaking, than the rest of us. Let's suppose they are indeed better judges of moral truth. It doesn't yet follow that anyone should be treated as an Authority-with-a-capital-'A'.

'Playing God'

Many will reject this, of course. Some will point an accusatory finger and say, 'You believe *you* should make your *own* judgement about what's right and what's wrong? The arrogance! You are playing God!'

But actually, like it or not, playing God is unavoidable. For how am I to know to which religious book, which religion, which religious sect and which interpreter of its sacred texts I am supposed to listen? Those who defer to religious Authority can pretend, if they like, that these judgements don't have to be made. But they cannot be avoided. Even just sticking with the religious authority with which I was raised requires that I make them. And they are *moral* judgements. They involve the question, '*Ought* I to follow the moral advice I'm being given?' However we're raised, we inevitably have to rely on our own moral compass – our own sense of right and wrong – in weighing up to whom we should listen and whether or not to accept the moral advice we are given. Like it or not, we *have* to 'play God'.

Those who say 'The arrogance! You're playing God!' deceive themselves if they suppose they're not playing God themselves. Moral responsibility is like a boomerang. You can try and throw it to someone else if you like – but you'll find that, in the end, it always comes back to you.

That's why you can't absolve yourself of responsibility for having committed some atrocity by pointing out that the moral Authority to which you defer said you should do it. If Stalin, the Pope, an Ayatollah or even the voice of 'God' in your head tells you to go out and kill the unbelievers, and you obey, you're still culpable.

Actually, it would come as something of a relief to me if I could hand over responsibility for making moral decisions to someone else. It's a responsibility that weighs heavily on my shoulders. How convenient it would be if, whenever I was faced with a moral decision, I could transfer the responsibility for making it to an 'expert'. Unfortunately, I can't.[2]

Kant Vindicated

If the argument sketched out above is cogent, then Kant is essentially correct.[3] When it comes to morality, it turns out that there is *a* sense in which the self is sovereign and autonomous. Given the boomerang-like quality of the responsibility for making moral judgements, it's actually *impossible* for us to do what those at the Authoritarian end of the Liberal/Authoritarian scale would like us to do: to wholly, or even largely, hand over responsibility for judging what's right and what's wrong to some external Authority. We may turn to others for advice and inspiration, of course. No doubt that's often wise. But the responsibility for questioning and judging whether or not it's advice that *ought* to be followed remains with us.

Given that each of us is going to have to take on this responsibility, like it or not, wouldn't it be a good idea to get individuals to recognize they have it? Wouldn't it also be a good idea to make sure they have the intellectual and emotional maturity to discharge it adequately? That kind of maturity is developed by a Liberal approach to moral and religious education, not an Authoritarian one.

The Authority of a Religious Text

Many religions are based around sacred texts – texts that in many cases are supposed to embody the word of God. But isn't the idea that there are such texts incompatible with a Liberal, Enlightened approach to moral education? Surely, to teach pupils that, say, the Bible is the word of God just *is* to teach them that they must defer unquestioningly and uncritically to it. But if this is true, then surely an Enlightened, Liberal approach to religious education is after all *incompatible with any religion based around a sacred text.*

Not so. A religious school might say to its pupils, 'We believe this text is the word of God. We believe that the moral code it presents is the one we should follow. But we don't want you unquestioningly and uncritically to accept this. We will explain why we think you should believe what we believe. But the decision whether or not to believe is ultimately yours, not ours, to make. It's a decision we want you to make only after careful, critical reflection.' This sort of attitude could quite consistently be adopted by a school like Liberalia High, for example.

The Bible, The Koran, The Bhagavad-Gita and so on are all extraordinarily rich and thought-provoking texts. No doubt all deserve close scrutiny. Perhaps one of these texts really is uniquely the word of God himself – it's 'authoritative' in that sense.

But we can accept that a particular text embodies the word of God without insisting that it be accepted as Authoritative with a capital 'A'. To insist that one particular religious text must be accepted more or less unquestioningly is to overlook the fact that each of us must ultimately figure out for ourselves which, if any, text to accept, which interpretation of the text we should listen to, and so on. The responsibility for making these moral judgements is unavoidable. Like it or not, it rests with the individual.

The Authority of Parents, Judges and Policemen

Here's another way in which we use the term 'authority'. Someone may be an authority because they are the legitimate wielder of a certain *power*. Take judges and policemen. Both have a certain expertise and training, and so qualify as authorities in the expertise sense of the word. But they are also authorities in the sense that they possess certain powers over the rest of us – the power to lock us up or punish us when we do wrong.

Parents also have this kind of authority. They're permitted, indeed expected, to discipline their children when they misbehave.

The existence of this sort of 'authority' is undoubtedly a good thing. Without a police force or a legal system we would immediately find ourselves in deep trouble. For the proper functioning of a society we need rules. We also need people who are empowered to enforce those rules. If rules and regulations can't be enforced, there's not much point having them.

But the need for authorities in this sense is entirely compatible with the Liberal approach to moral education. We've already seen that Liberals are concerned with freedom of thought, not freedom of action. Liberals can acknowledge that we need rules and that children need firm boundaries. And of course they can acknowledge that those rules and boundaries require authorities to enforce them: the authority invested in parents, teachers, headmasters and headmistresses, policemen and judges.

How Authoritarians Take Advantage of the Ambiguity of 'Authority'

Many people, struck by the rise in crime and delinquency over the last fifty years or so, are now calling for a return to 'authority'. However, not all of these fans of 'authority' are Authoritarian with a capital 'A'. They merely want respect for judges, teachers, parents, discipline and the rule of law. Of course, Liberals can be all in favour of these things too. Unfortunately, Liberals tend to get caricatured as being against *all* authority – that's quite unfair.

Also, because it's often unclear what people mean when they say they want more 'respect for authority', it's easy for some Authoritarians to take advantage of the confusion and pretend that there is widespread agreement that we need a more Authoritarian approach to moral education.

The moral is that we need to be very clear what we mean when conceding that 'authority' is a good thing. Otherwise we may find ourselves unwittingly dragged aboard the Authoritarian bandwagon. Liberals should start insisting that proponents of 'authority' spell out *exactly* what it is they are promoting – Authority, authority, or a combination of the two. Let's be clear that we can say 'yes' to authority while issuing an unequivocal 'no' to Authority-with-a-captial-'A'.

Liberalism and Selfish Individualism

This chapter has already busted two anti-Liberal myths – the myth that Liberals are intent on undermining the 'authority' of judges, police, teachers and parents to enforce rules and discipline, and the myth that Liberals must deny the obvious fact that some people are moral 'authorities' in the sense that they're morally wiser than the rest of us. The truth, contrary to what some Authoritarians would have you believe, is that Liberals need not do either of those things. Liberals may reject Authority. They can still confidently embrace these other forms of 'authority'. It's time both these anti-Liberal myths were nailed.

Let's now clear up yet another poisonous misconception: that Liberalism *must inevitably promote a culture of shallow, selfish, materialist individualism.*

The West is often accused of being unhealthily consumerist and individualist, and with some justification. No doubt many Westerners are rather too focused on self-gratification and the acquisition of material goods – on getting their hands on the latest phone, the flashiest TV, the newest car and the biggest house – often at the expense of more important things in life. Let's agree this selfish, grasping, materialistic inclination needs combating.

As I say, it's often assumed Liberals must inevitably promote this hedonistic tendency. 'So you think individuals should be free to make up their *own* minds about morality and religion?' ask the critics. 'You think *they* should get to make those judgements? Then you're encouraging them to do whatever *they* want, to do whatever feels good to *them*, to satisfy their *own* immediate, shallow selfish desires at the expense of everyone and everything else.'

But this is untrue. It takes only a moment's thought to realize that encouraging individuals to think and make their own judgements about right and wrong is not to encourage them to believe or do whatever they believe is in their own interest. To say to an individual 'You must judge what is right and wrong' is *not* to say 'You must judge on a wholly shallow, materialistic, self-serving basis'.

Yes we should teach young people to think independently and encourage them to make their own moral judgements. But we can do that while at the same time explaining to them, clearly and powerfully, why the relentless pursuit of self-gratification at the expense of everything else is ultimately an unsatisfying and, more importantly, a morally reprehensible way to live. A Liberal Christian might even choose to give specifically *religious* arguments against that sort of lifestyle. In short, *Liberals are just as free to combat the culture of selfish individualism as are Authoritarians*.

When it comes to resisting this culture, the difference between the Liberal and the Authoritarian lies in their method. The Authoritarian will want the individual to accept the wrongness of selfish individualism more-or-less on the say-so of some Authority. Liberals, on the other hand, will feel themselves under an obligation to engage in free and open discussion, to explain and make their case as best they can.

And yet, despite the fact that Liberals are just as free to combat selfish individualism as Authoritarians, Liberals are often caricatured by their opponents as being the friends of selfish individualism. In fact this is yet another popular anti-Liberal smear.

'What If They End Up Believing the Wrong Thing?'

The Liberal approach does, of course, come with a risk attached. If we allow – even encourage – people to think for themselves, what if they then end up with mistaken beliefs? What if little Johnny ends up convincing himself that mugging old ladies and vandalizing phone boxes is right? Who is going to correct him? And how are we to protect ourselves against such people?

This worry might tempt some back in the direction of Authority-based moral education, which simply tells children what they must believe about right and wrong.

The risk exists, but we shouldn't let Authoritarians exaggerate it. First of all, remember that Liberals can physically restrain little Johnny, and punish his bad behaviour. Some might think this involves the Liberal in a contradiction: 'If you restrain him and impose your authority on him, then you are yourself being Authoritarian, and thus a hypocrite!'

But there's no hypocrisy involved here. First of all, remember that the Liberal approach to moral education is about *freedom of thought, not freedom of action*. It is entirely consistent with rules, discipline, the authority of parents, teachers and police to control and punish bad behaviour. What characterizes Liberals is their opposition to Authority with a capital 'A'. Liberals are not committed to letting little Johnny *do* whatever he likes. They are committed only to allowing him freedom of thought and expression.

Secondly, how likely is it, in fact, that a pupil raised within a Liberal school will end up with such mistaken beliefs? Remember that the idea is not completely to *ignore* morality, so that the child is forced to conjure up their own moral code out of nothing, all by themselves, without any guidance at all. Liberals can teach right from wrong. We've seen that they are even free to teach solid, traditional Christian or Muslim or other religious values. It's the way in which those values are communicated that matters. The Liberal will encourage the child to think independently. That doesn't mean without guidance or correction.

But in any case, even if, after, say, a Liberal Christian upbringing, a child does end up convinced that there's nothing morally wrong with mugging old ladies, surely it is better that individuals make wrong judgements than that some Authority does on their behalf. An individual educated in the way the Liberal suggests may end up disagreeing with us on some key moral issue. But, as was mentioned in chapter four, at least we will be able to enter into a rational discussion with them about the pros and cons of both their and our position. Those who have handed over responsibility for making such decisions to some Authority, on the other hand, are likely to be beyond rational debate.

Mistakes are inevitable. What's important is that we foster a culture in which mistakes can be corrected – where the opportunity exists for us to correct each other. That culture is a Liberal culture, not an Authoritarian one.

The Liberal Response to Authoritarians in their Midst

But perhaps there does still remain an inconsistency in the Liberal position. How should a Liberal society respond to an Authoritarian movement that develops in its own midst? Suppose, for example, that, within a Liberal society, a religious cult emerges that's highly intolerant of its own members thinking critically and independently. This cult demands that its followers accept unquestioningly the pronouncements of its leader.

If this society is Liberal, and promotes freedom of thought and expression, isn't it going to have to tolerate the Authoritarian attitudes of this cult? But then, paradoxically, it ends up condoning the cult's Authoritarianism. If, on the other hand, this Liberal society acts to prevent the cult behaving in an Authoritarian way, isn't it guilty of being Authoritarian *itself*? Either way, it ends up being downright inconsistent. It preaches Liberalism while practising, or at least condoning, Authoritarianism.

Again, I don't believe there's any inconsistency here.

If this Liberal society believes the Authoritarian cult within its midst is comparatively benign, it may tolerate it. A Liberal society can consistently allow its citizens to reject its Liberalism and even to argue publicly against it. It can respect its critics' freedom of thought and expression, even while trying rationally to persuade them that being Liberal is preferable. To tolerate dissent is not to embrace or condone the views of the dissenter. A consistent Liberal society will not demand that everyone unquestioningly accept that being Liberal is best, and gag all dissenters. That would indeed make them unacceptably Authoritarian.

If, on the other hand, this cult turns out to be brainwashing its members and perhaps instructing them to engage in violence, then the Liberal society in which the cult is embedded might well be justified in curtailing the cult's activities. In so doing, this society would indeed be applying its authority, but we're now talking about authority with a small 'a', not a capital 'A'. We are talking about restricting behaviour, not thought.[4]

Liberals are often accused of inconsistency. And it may be true that some of the views that go by the name 'liberal' are indeed inconsistent. But I don't yet see that any such inconsistency affects Liberalism-with-a-capital-'L'.

There is one way in which Liberals might be inconsistent, of course. As we just acknowledged, a Liberal who encourages independent critical thought about everything *except their own Liberal attitudes*, which they insist should be accepted on their say so, would clearly be a hypocrite. A consistent Liberal will be prepared to subject, and allow others to subject, even their Liberal values to close critical scrutiny. But then there's no reason why they can't do that.

Conclusion

Many are now calling for greater discipline from schools and parents. Many want greater respect for 'authority'. In particular, they want children to acknowledge and respect the authority of parents, teachers, police, and so on. Many would like their children to have a religious upbringing. They would like their children to acknowledge that there may be much to learn, both morally and spiritually, from others, including, perhaps, their religious leaders.

As I hope is now becoming clear, *all of this is entirely consistent with the kind of Liberal approach to moral education outlined in chapter three.* None of this requires that we give up on Kant's vision of Enlightenment, on which individuals are encouraged to think critically and for themselves. None of this requires that we return to Authority-based moral and religious education of the sort that was dominant up until the 1960s.

Indeed, we've seen in this chapter that we *cannot* do what those who favour Authority-based moral education require us to do: to hand over responsibility for making moral judgements to some external Authority. The responsibility for thinking about and judging what is right and what is wrong has a boomerang-like quality – like it or not, it always comes back to you.

Still, the fact is that very many people – not just hard-line religious conservatives – now say we have travelled too far in the Liberal direction. We need to move back in the direction of Authority with a capital 'A'. Why?

Probably the most popular justification for returning to more Authority-based values education is that our excessively Liberal approach to moral education has supposedly produced a *moral malaise*. It's to this malaise that we now turn our attention.

Six

The Moral Malaise

We in the West are in trouble. Deep trouble. Or at least that's what we're regularly told. Social and political commentators are voicing the gravest of concerns about threats to the fabric of our society.

The popular analogy is with an illness. Only the disease that supposedly afflicts the West is not medical, but moral. We're suffering from what's often called a 'moral malaise'. Americans consistently tell pollsters that 'moral decay' or 'moral decline' is one of the nation's severest problems, and the concern grows more pronounced year on year. Shelves of hand-wringing books and articles are published annually on the Where-did-we-go-wrong? and What-is-to-be-done? theme.

Some believe the situation is now so bad that, unless we act quickly, the illness will become terminal. America, it's claimed, is going 'to hell in a hand basket'. The once firm moral foundations that underpinned Western society are rapidly dissolving. Contemporary Western civilization will go the same way as the Roman, Greek and Egyptian civilizations that preceded it. Here, for example, is Doggett (2001), a US radio talk-show host, predicting the end-of-the-world-as-we-know-it:

> ... there is a sickness in our body politic. There is a sickness in our
> soul. If we don't declare war on our moral malaise, we are going
> to die as a people. Communists, terrorists or drug lords will not

destroy us. We will fall, like all great civilizations before us, because we have become rotten to the core.

Of course, not everyone shares this apocalyptic vision. Opinions differ over just how serious the cracks in the social fabric really are. Still, there's an emerging consensus that, morally speaking, something has gone very wrong indeed. As Himmelfarb, one of America's best-known neo-conservative thinkers, points out,

[i]t is not only conservatives ... who now deplore the breakdown of the family; liberals do as well. [Few today] seriously doubt the inadequacy of education at all levels, or the fragility of communal ties, or the coarsening and debasement of the culture, or the 'defining down' of morality, public and private. It is no mean achievement to have reached at least this point of consensus (Himmelfarb, quoted in Jacoby (2001: 163).

What does the malaise involve? There would seem to be at least three key ingredients.

First, the West has become much more *secularized*. Many mourn the decline in religious tradition and authority that has taken place, particularly since the 1960s. It's said that, as we have lost these old traditions and authorities, so we have also lost our moral bearings. Secondly, the West has experienced a huge rise in crime, and also an accompanying shift in our sexual attitudes, over the last half-century or so. Here would seem to be hard evidence of a loss of values. Thirdly, we have seen the rise of something called *relativism*, particularly in our schools and colleges. Let's take a closer look at each of these three ingredients in turn.

Secularization

There's widespread agreement that one of the critical factors in producing the current sorry state of affairs is the rapid secularization of society that has taken place particularly over the last 50 years or so. Here, for example, is Sacks (1997: 260–261), the UK's chief rabbi, lamenting what he believes we have lost.

A vision once guided us, one that we loosely call the Judeo-Christian tradition ... It did not answer all questions. ... But it gave us moral habits. It gave us a framework of virtue. It embodied ideals. It emphasized the value of institutions – the family, the school, the community – as vehicles through which one generation hands on its ideals to the next. In its broad outlines it was shared by rich and poor alike. ... You could catch traces of it from pub to pulpit to cricket matches. It bound us together as a nation gave an entire society its bearings. That tradition has been comprehensively displaced.

Sacks is, of course, correct that much of the West is more secular than it was. Creeping secularization has been around for centuries. But in the middle of the twentieth century the rate of secularization dramatically accelerated. The graphs show, for example, that in the UK from the mid-1960s onwards, church attendance nose-dived.

What has this to do with the current malaise? In fact, the decline of established religion is commonly thought to have had three critical effects.

First, as religious belief has waned, so society has become increasingly fragmented. Our shared religious traditions once framed a way of life. As Sacks just put it, they 'bound us together as a nation'. We collectively turned to religion to mark the great rites of passage, including birth, death, weddings. From the weekly attendance at church or synagogue to the yearly calendar of festivals, our years were marked out by religious practices and routines that drew us together both physically and spiritually. Our religious community also provided us with a rich network of moral and spiritual support when times were hard. We felt we 'belonged'. As a result of the collapse of the old religious framework, society has become atomized. Instead of a community, we have became a loose collection of free-floating individuals. We no longer feel any particularly deep sense of allegiance to or connection with those around us. It's this atomization that Himmelfarb has in mind when she talks of the 'fragility of communal ties'.

Secondly, it's thought that with the loss of the traditional religious framework we have also lost all sense of there being a wider purpose or meaning to our lives. It was within the religious framework that deeper questions about why we are here, how we should live our lives and where we will eventually end up were once asked. As that framework has collapsed, we have, so the complaint goes, ceased asking such questions, let alone trying to answer them. We have become shallow and materialistic.

Thirdly, and most importantly, it's claimed that with the loss of religious tradition we have lost our moral compass. The old religious framework did at least give us clear unambiguous guidance on how to behave. It drilled us in certain well-defined moral habits, such as honesty, integrity, self-control, respect. As a result of rapid secularization, claims Sacks, these old virtues were no longer communicated from generation to generation in the same sure-footed way. During the 1960s and 1970s, more and more of us began to view the traditional ways of teaching right and wrong as antiquated, authoritarian and oppressive. Rather than deferring to some external moral authority and tradition, we were increasingly abandoned to make up our own minds about right and wrong.

As a result, from the mid-1960s onwards, young people were raised more and more within a moral vacuum. Moral education, both in homes and schools, largely disappeared. With no external moral authority to which they might turn for guidance, individuals grew up thinking they were their own ultimate arbiter of right or wrong. Morality, to borrow a popular phrase, became 'privatized'.

Crime, Youth and Sex

Crime

At the same time as traditional, religious sources of moral authority went into decline, cracks began to appear in the social fabric. Perhaps the most serious of these cracks is a rise in crime. Statistics on crime are notoriously difficult to compare, but there is little doubt that in the last 50 years or so much of the West has seen a substantial increase in the levels of criminality.

The statistics do appear to support the view that the UK experienced comparatively low rates of crime in the 100 years running up to the 1960s, at which point the situation changed markedly. In 1950 about half a million crimes were reported. Now about six million crimes are recorded each year. The US also appears to have experienced a rapid rise in crime. For example, between 1960 and 1992, US citizens experienced a five-fold increase in the rate of violent crime (murder, rape, robbery, aggravated assault) (Himmelfarb 1995: epilogue).

Crime statistics should be treated with care. Crime is measured in different ways at different times, making precise comparisons difficult. The figures tend to reflect reported crime, which may not correlate with the true level. And what counts as a crime at one time may not at another (drink-driving, for example, is illegal now, but wasn't in the 1950s; homosexuality was illegal then, but isn't now). But, even having admitted all this, it does seem that both the US and the UK have witnessed a significant rise in crime since the mid-1960s.

Youth

As we all know, every generation is regarded by its immediate predecessor as somewhat suspect. The eternal complaint is that 'young people today are ...' well, you know the rest – some combination of feckless, lazy, rude, greedy, shallow, materialistic, arrogant, lacking in respect for their elders, and so on. Robert Baden-Powell, who founded the Scout movement at the beginning of the twentieth century, complained that far too many boys were 'drifting towards hooliganism and bad citizenship for want of hands to guide them'.[1] The same complaint is made today.

But while each generation seems to have an in-built bias against its own young, the fact is that there is, nevertheless, evidence that today's young really are less well behaved than were their grandparents at the same age. In the US, schools that, half a century ago, had little more to worry about than the occasional truant now have to employ armed, uniformed security guards and metal detectors to remove knives and firearms (though, having said that, there does also appear to have been a significant reduction in serious violent crime in US schools since 1994).[2]

Sex

Attitudes to sex have changed too, particularly during the late 1960s and early 1970s. Take, for example, our attitudes to pre-marital sex. In 1969, 21.4% of respondents to a Gallup poll said pre-marital sex was 'not wrong'. In 1973, 43% said it was 'not wrong'. That's a fairly radical shift in attitudes in just four years.[3] Changing attitudes have been accompanied by changes in behaviour. Consider out-of-wed-lock births, for example. In England and Wales, between 1960 and 1992 the rate rose from five per cent to 32 per cent. There has been a similar rise in the US (Himmelfarb 1995: 222–224). Statistics suggest that in 1970, 85 per cent of children under 18 lived with two parents, compared to only 72 per cent now. Divorce caused 37 per cent of these one-parent households, and in one third of cases the parent was never married.[4]

Some might say, 'So what? What's the problem with pre-marital sex? Weren't we excessively prudish about sex pre-1960? Isn't there something to be said for at least some sexual experimentation before marriage? At least couples can now discover whether they're sexually compatible before it's too late.' Some might also welcome the rise in the divorce rate: 'All that has happened is that deeply unhappy couples that were previously compelled by social pressures to stay together are now free to part company. Thank goodness for that.' They may also insist that one-parent families are not necessarily a bad thing: 'What's wrong with single-parent families as such? Why assume that a one-parent family is any better or worse than the traditional wedded two-parent unit?'

We shouldn't dismiss these responses out of hand. But it remains clear that at least some shifts in sexual behaviour since the mid-1960s have had a detrimental effect. Surely no one would welcome the very sharp rise in unwanted teenage pregnancies that has taken place over the last half-century or so. This is at least partly down to the fact that teenagers are having sex earlier and more often than they used to, and this, in turn, has come about at least in part because of our more relaxed and permissive attitudes towards sex.

There's also fairly good evidence that the huge, post-1960s boom in single-parent families is linked to the sharp rise in crime and delinquency mentioned earlier. Studies suggest that the off-spring of single parents are more likely to be delinquent and offend. While poverty may also be a factor (single-parent homes also tend to be poorer homes), there's evidence that even when poverty is taken into consideration, children from single-parent homes have significantly greater problems with criminality. While the evidence may not be absolutely conclusive,[5] it does lend con-siderable support to the claim that the dramatic rise in single-parent families has played at least a causal role in generating the rise of crime.[6]

The Rise of Relativism

So let's acknowledge that Western societies have experienced some important changes for the worse over the past fifty years or so. Why are these changes happening? We are now approaching what many consider to be the dark heart of the malaise. One word is pretty much guaranteed to crop up whenever moral decay is discussed. That word is 'relativism'.

Relativism is the view that what's true for one person or culture may be false for another. There's no absolute moral truth, just differing opinions, all of which are equally valid.

Here's an analogy. No doubt you have heard of Witchetty grubs: those huge larvae from the Australian outback. The grubs are eaten live by aboriginal Australians. Some consider them delicious. But of course, for most Westerners, the prospect of eating huge, squirming larvae gives them the screaming heebie-jeebies. In a recent edition of the UK TV show, *I'm A Celebrity, Get Me Out Of Here*, two celebrities required to eat several live Witchetty grubs said it was one of the most disgusting things they had ever had to do (one said it was 'worse than childbirth'). They certainly didn't find Witchetty grubs delicious.

Now ask yourself, what's the truth about Witchetty grubs? Are they delicious, or aren't they? Surely, there's no right answer to that question. *Being delicious* is not an objective property of things in the way that, say, *being square* or *being made out of atoms* is. Deliciousness is not a quality that's 'out there', independently of us. Rather, it's a property rooted in our own subjective reactions to things.

But then there is no objective truth about whether or not Witchetty grubs are delicious. The truth about the deliciousness of Witchetty grubs is relative. From the point of view of some aboriginal Australians, it's true that Witchetty grubs are delicious; from the point of view of most Westerners, it's false. In this case, what's true and what's false depends on your point of view. Ultimately it boils down to a difference in taste or opinion.

Now the kind of moral relativism on which the moral malaise is blamed holds that *moral properties are similarly relative properties*. They are properties rooted not in objective reality, but in our subjective reactions to it. Take, for example, the practice of female circumcision widely discussed in the media a few years ago. Many Westerners are horrified by it. The practice does, after all, result in a loss of sexual pleasure for the woman concerned, and it's forced on young children without their consent. Many in the West argue that it should be stopped. But of course those who practise female circumcision (in, for example, Somalia, where it is the norm) think it's entirely morally proper. So who's right?

According to the relativist, *both* points of view are correct. Relative to most Westerners it's 'true' that female circumcision is wrong. But, relative to most Somalians, it's 'true' that it's morally correct.

At this point some might be tempted to ask: but what is true *really*? Setting aside the fact that people hold these differing points of view, which point of view is actually correct? According to the moral relativist, there is no such thing as objective, non-relative moral truth. That's their point. Moral truths are relative. Morality, like deliciousness, is ultimately a matter of taste or preference or sentiment, not a matter of objective fact.

The 'Politically Correct' Argument for Relativism

Many are drawn to relativism, especially moral relativism. People sometimes assume that, if we are to be good, tolerant, open-minded liberals, we really have no choice but to embrace relativism. Here's a popular line of argument.

> In the past, we Westerners have forced our own moral standards on others. We have coerced them into accepting our own views about right and wrong. We have assumed we must be right and they must be wrong. But now we are rightly beginning to question our own moral infallibility. We now know we can learn much from other cultures, both morally and spiritually. We also realize not only that our own moral point of view is just one among many, but also that it is itself constantly shifting and changing.
> But isn't this just to recognize that moral relativism is true? For us, say, female circumcision is wrong. For other cultures it's right. There's no further, objective 'fact of the matter' about whether it's really right or wrong. When it comes to morality, truth is relative. Which is exactly why it would be wrong for us to impose our own perspective on another culture.

Many are persuaded by this kind of argument. In fact, in some quarters, to reject relativism is to risk being branded 'politically incorrect', a cultural imperialist, or worse (suggest that those Somalians who practise female circumcision are doing something wrong, for example, and you may find yourself accused of racism). Those who reject relativism may find themselves portrayed as jack-booted bullies intent on ramming their moral beliefs down every-one else's throats.

As a consequence, a culture of non-judgementalism has emerged. Many relativists insist that, as there's no objective fact of the matter about whether, say, polygamy or female circumcision is wrong, so it's wrong of us to judge. Those of us who point an accusatory finger at the moral standards of other cultures and say 'That's wrong' should desist.

This, it's widely supposed, is where things have fundamentally gone wrong. Under the guise of 'tolerance' and 'open-mindedness', relativism has spread out into Western culture. Teachers educated in the relativist climate of the 1960s and 1970s have gone on to foster relativist attitudes in the classroom. Because they no longer feel comfortable about 'imposing' an established moral code on children – because they feel it would be 'politically incorrect' to do so – teachers have increasingly opted either to ignore moral education altogether, or else have turned moral education into an exercise in 'values clarification' in which children are encouraged to invent their own values. Here's a fairly typical complaint from Bennett (2002), a US philosophy professor who later became US Secretary of Education:

> Teaching children about morality – making meaningful concepts like right and wrong, good and evil – is imperative. It also is a duty that we have shirked all too often in the past 40 years. Concepts like cultural relativism, multiculturalism and values clarification, in which students are encouraged to identify and 'clarify' their own beliefs, have spilled over from our colleges and universities into our elementary schools classrooms … This must stop.

Relativism, it's often argued, has also poisoned our homes. Parents no longer feel they have the right to force their own values on their children. Adults, no longer confident in either their own moral authority or the objectivity of their moral judgements, are standing back and allowing their children to run amok.

Rampant Relativism and Non-Judgementalism

Indeed, relativism is now widely considered to be the dominant pop-philosophy of the West. The American academic Bloom (1988: 25) writes that

> [t]here is one thing a professor can be absolutely certain of: almost every student entering university believes, or says he believes, that truth is relative.

A similar seismic cultural shift is reported in the UK. Marianne Talbot, a lecturer in philosophy, Brasenose College, Oxford, reports about her students that many have been taught to think their opinion is no better than anyone else's, that there is no truth, only truth-for-me. I come across this relativist view constantly – in exams, in discussion and in tutorials – and I find it frightening: to question it amounts, in the eyes of the young, to the belief that it is permissible to impose your views on others (quoted in Phillips 1996: 221).

William Bennett (quoted above) concurs. He says,

the answers I started to get from students in the '60s were, 'I think each person should do his own thing. I mean if they want to do something, who am I to say something's right, who am I to say something's wrong?'[7]

Richard Hoggart has commented on a similar rise in relativism and non-judgementalism among the working-class inhabitants of his own British hometown. While criticizing a book espousing traditional virtues, he nevertheless admits:

[i]n Hunslet, a working-class district of Leeds, within which I was brought up, old people will still enunciate, as guides to living, the moral rules they learned at Sunday School and Chapel. Then they almost always add, these days: 'But it's only my opinion, of course'. A late-twentieth-century insurance clause, a recognition that times have changed towards the always shiftingly relativist. In that same council estate, any idea of parental guidance has in many homes been lost. Most of the children there live in a violent, jungle world (quoted in Himmelfarb 1995: 241).

Himmelfarb (1999: 122) supplies another illustration:

Robert Simon, a professor of philosophy, reports that while none of his students denies the reality of the Holocaust, an increasing number do worse: they acknowledge the fact, even deplore it, but cannot bring themselves to condemn it morally. 'Of course I dislike the Nazis,' one student comments, 'but who is to say they are morally wrong.' They make similar observations about apartheid, slavery, and ethnic cleansing. To pass judgement, they fear, is to be moral 'absolutist', and having been taught that there are no absolutes, they now see any judgement as arbitrary, intolerant, and authoritarian.

The former Archbishop of Canterbury, Dr Carey (1996), in his House of Lords address, also warned of the danger

> of moral relativism and privatized morality. There is a widespread tendency to view what is good and right as a matter of private taste and individual opinion only. Under this tendency, God is banished to the realm of the private hobby and religion becomes a particular activity for those who happen to have a taste for it.

It's this rampant relativism that, more than anything, now gets the blame for the moral malaise. If morality is nothing more than a matter of personal choice or preference, then teenage thugs can steal, vandalize and assault with impunity, confident that no one has the right to gainsay them. Richard Lamm, former governor of Colorado, sums up the devastation he believes relativism has wrought:

> In attempting to be tolerant, we have wiped out all the rules. ... It is hard these days to find a standard to which we can hold people. Everything is relative. Our moral compass gyrates wildly. There is no true north. But history shows us this is not a sustainable trait.[8]

So popular is this diagnosis that whenever an example of immorality crops up, the knee-jerk response of many is immediately to blame moral relativism. Take the recent outrage at Abu Ghraib, where Iraqis were tortured by US personnel. What caused this moral breakdown? The instinctive reaction of Richard Land, head of the Southern Baptist Convention's Ethics & Religious Liberty Commission, was to suspect the influence of moral relativism:

> This is not a breakdown in the system. This reflects a breakdown in society. These people's moral compass didn't work for some reason. My guess is because they've been infected with relativism.[9]

Yes, crime needs to be tackled. Many would say religion needs to be resurrected. But what, above all, gets the blame for the awful situation in which we now find ourselves is relativism. The decline of traditional, religious values and values education has in large part been brought about by this poisonous doctrine. The old fashioned position that some moral claims are objectively 'true' and others 'false' has been replaced by the view that all moral points of view are equally 'valid'. The result has been a moral catastrophe. Even the new Pontiff has made it clear that fighting the battle against the 'dictatorship of relativism' is one of his highest priorities:

> We are moving towards a dictatorship of relativism which does not recognize anything as for certain and which has as its highest goal one's own ego and one's own desires (Ratzinger 2005).

Governments are now beginning to introduce educational and social policies deliberately designed to target relativism, particularly in schools. Take, for example, citizenship classes in the UK. When Nick Tate, head of the UK's SCAA (the UK body responsible for devising and assessing the national curriculum), introduced compulsory classes in citizenship for all pupils attending state-funded schools, he was explicit that one of his chief concerns was to 'slay the dragon of relativism'.[10]

But how, precisely, do we slay the dragon of relativism?

Is Religion the Cure?

Some believe the cure is essentially simple. More religion. If it was the loss of religion that produced the malaise, then the cure is straightforward: bring it back. Let's have more faith schools, more religious programming and more religious figures speaking out on the issues of the day. Let's push religion back onto the political agenda. We can regenerate Western culture by reinfusing it with religion. In the UK, Prime Minister Tony Blair's enthusiasm for 'faith' schools is undoubtedly partly motivated by a sense that religion must be at least part of the cure.

But there is an obvious problem with the thought that religious belief is the solution: 96 per cent of Americans claim to believe in God. Not only do they believe in God, many of them also go to church: 60 per cent of them say they attend church at least once a month. Compare that with Britain, where in 1980 only 14 per cent claimed to attend church regularly and in 1999 just 7 per cent did.[11] And yet, while Western Europe and Canada are far more secular than the US, they don't appear to be suffering a deeper moral malaise. Quite the reverse, it seems (see, for example, Paul 2005). Despite the fact that, in the US, almost *everyone* believes in God, the US has far more serious problems with crime and delinquency. The suggestion that we can cure our moral malaise simply by bringing back religious belief and practice is clearly over-simplistic. In the US, it never went away.

The *Wrong Sort* of Religion?

Maybe Americans now have the *wrong sort* of religious belief? That's what some neo-conservatives suggest. Take Himmelfarb (1999: 120), for example:

> Even when they complain about the 'moral decline' of the country (which they continue to do, in very large numbers), they offer little resistance to manifestations of that decline. They believe in God, but they believe even more in the autonomy of the individual. They confess that they find it difficult to judge what is moral or immoral even for themselves, still more for others. Thus they habitually take refuge in such equivocations as 'Who is to say what is right or wrong?'

According to Himmelfarb, the kind of religious belief prevalent in the US is highly relativistic and non-judgemental. A person's religious and moral beliefs, it's supposed, are a wholly private matter. There is an unwillingness to foist them on others, be it in the home, in school or in society at large. As a consequence, even the children of religious, church-going parents lack proper moral guidance. It's also claimed that the God of a typical US 'liberal' is very undemanding. As one reviewer of Himmelfarb's *One Nation, Two Cultures* puts it:

> The nation's religiosity ... is a mile wide and an inch deep. Ninety-six percent of Americans claim to believe in God, but if that God is

the one presented by the liberal churches, He is a God who did not reveal much, and does not really demand much of us (Johansen 2000).

Back to Authority with a Capital 'A'

What, then, is the cure? By far the most popular view is that we need to rehabilitate, not just religion, but 'religious authority'.

But what sort of authority? In chapter five we saw that there are several different forms of 'authority', many of which are clearly a good idea: the authority of policemen, judges and parents to correct and punish bad behaviour, for example, is clearly something we need to rely on. But it's not just that brand of 'authority' that those complaining most loudly of a moral malaise typically want to bring back. What was lost with the Enlightenment and the 1960s was religious, Authority-based values education. It was the loss of religious Authority with a capital 'A' that caused the rise of relativism and the moral malaise. It's Authority with a capital 'A' they want to reinstate.

Take the UK's chief rabbi, Jonathan Sacks, for example. We saw in chapter one that Sacks places the blame for the malaise on the Enlightenment, and particularly on Kant. To repeat, Sacks (1997: 176) says that,

> according to Kant ... [t]o do something because others do, or because of habit or custom or even Divine Command, is to accept an external authority over the one sovereign territory that is truly our own: our own choices. The moral being for Kant is by definition an autonomous being, a person who accepts no other authority than the self. By the 1960s this was beginning to gain hold as an educational orthodoxy. The task of education is not to hand on a tradition but to enhance the consciousness of choice.

It's this Kantian rejection of any external moral Authority that might decide right and wrong for us – this insistence on the autonomy of the individual – that is the root cause of our problems. It's here that we find the origin of today's relativism. For to teach in accordance with this Kantian doctrine, says Sacks (1997), requires 'non-judgementalism and relativism on the part of the teacher'. The results have been disastrous. It's time to bring, not just rules and discipline, but also moral Authority with a capital 'A', back into both our homes and our schools.

The British columnist, author and social commentator Phillips (1996: 189) concurs. 'It seems reasonable,' she says, 'to regard the Enlightenment as the defining moment for the collapse of external authority.' The problem with Enlightenment thinking, argues Phillips (1996: 28), is that

> instead of authority being located 'out there' in a body of knowledge handed down through the centuries, we have repositioned it 'in here' within each child.

Because each individual 'has become their own individual arbiter of conduct' so relativism and the view that 'no-one else [is] permitted to pass judgement' have become the norm (Phillips 1996: 116). And so, as a direct consequence of Enlightenment thinking,

> [w]ithin three centuries ... morality became a matter of individual will, preference, emotion or decision. ... The concepts of right and wrong became meaningless because they no longer applied to objective principles. There were no moral standards anymore, only choices (Phillips 1996: 197).

So, according to Sacks and Phillips, it's the Enlightenment-induced collapse of external moral Authority with a capital 'A' that lies behind the rise of relativism. In other words, it's *Kant and his Liberal disciples who are, ultimately, to blame for our moral malaise.*

Jeff Jacoby, columnist with the *Boston Globe*, supplies a similar diagnosis in response to the question 'What went wrong?', although he shifts the blame to a more recent epoch: the 1960s.

> The conventional answer, especially among conservatives, is that the 1960s happened. Authority, tradition and sexual restraint were undone by a tsunami of social shocks: Civil rights, the pill, television, the anti-war movement, the swelling of the welfare

state, the Baby Boom. Any one of these developments would have changed American life. All of them together fuelled a cultural revolution that profoundly altered American society, as the old culture based on moral authority gave way to a new one based on permissiveness (or 'tolerance'). In the new culture, traditional morality was no longer something to be enforced – not by government, not by civil society, not even by social pressure – but instead became a matter of 'personal preference'. And as moral authority yielded to moral autonomy, vice became almost as respectable as virtue. … [T]he old culture based on moral authority gave way to a new one based on permissiveness (or 'tolerance') (Jacoby 2001).

Again, the suggestion seems to be that it was not just the loss of authority with a small 'a' that caused the damage – the loss of rules and discipline – but the loss of Authority with a capital 'A': the freeing-up of individuals to make their own judgements. The move from moral Authority to moral autonomy resulted in the relativization of morality and its debasement into mere 'personal preference'. The cure, presumably, requires we now move in the opposite direction: from moral autonomy back to moral Authority.

But where do we begin? Many believe a good place to start would be with our children. Children – and perhaps even adults – need to understand that what is right and what is wrong is not a matter for them to decide. They must be encouraged to defer to those who know better – to some external moral Authority: to a parent, teacher, priest or a rabbi, and perhaps to a wider faith or other community.

But of course, this requires that we reject the Liberal approach to moral education that was advocated in chapter three. Indeed, many claim *it's precisely the Liberal approach to moral education that is to blame for the dire situation in which we now find ourselves.* They believe it was the Liberalizing of society and, more specifically, the Liberalizing of moral education that ultimately produced the rot.

Seven

Changes for the Good

In the previous chapter we looked at the claim, endlessly repeated by conservatives, that the West's moral malaise is a product of relativism, which is in turn a result of the rise of Liberal attitudes. Basically, it's Enlightenment and the 1960s that are to blame.

In this chapter, we'll see why relativism – and certainly that 'politically correct' brand of relativism on which the malaise gets blamed – *should* be rejected. But before we get to that, let's briefly examine the claim that, morally speaking, things really are much worse than they were fifty years ago. So often is this 'moral malaise' mantra repeated that it's easy to forget that there are, in fact, ways in which the moral attitudes of Westerners have substantially improved.

Take, for example, our attitudes towards racism and racial segregation. In the 1950s racist attitudes were rife. In the US, blacks were segregated from whites. This was considered by many to be entirely morally acceptable. Many considered it Biblically justified. Across much of the West, this situation has very substantially improved. Let's not forget that it was during the 1960s, in particular, that considerable progress was made in securing black people equal rights.

Or take our moral attitudes towards women. Until the 1950s, many communities across the West considered women second-class citizens. Women were forced to be financially dependent upon men, many of whom believed they had a moral right to treat their wives as little more than sexual and household serfs. Women were discouraged from working. While sons were expected to enter university, daughters were dissuaded from learning much more than housekeeping and some basic secretarial skills. Across all the major institutions, the levers of power lay firmly in the hands of men. This situation was, again, often religiously justified. The last 50 years or so have seen a very marked improvement in our attitudes. Women are now much closer to achieving genuine equality, and certainly they have a voice. It's ironic that many of those female social commentators who complain so loudly about the 'loss of values' over the last half-century are only now able to do so because of this revolution in our values.

Our attitudes towards homosexuality have also changed. In the 1950s, being a practising homosexual was a criminal offence. Someone suspected of being homosexual might be verbally abused, blackmailed, physically assaulted, prosecuted or worse. The justification for the discrimination against homosexuals was, of course, largely religious. As the old religious framework went into decline, so the morally bankrupt religious justifications for condemning the actively homosexual went with it. That has been a change for the better.

There has also been a very profound shift in our moral thinking about our environment and the other species that inhabit it. Young people in particular feel very strongly about the environment. Many recognize they have a moral obligation to protect it. Increasing numbers of them are also embracing vegetarianism. Again, they are doing so largely for moral reasons.

In short, let's not forget that many of the recent changes in our moral attitudes have been improvements. These improvements were largely brought about by Enlightened individuals who were prepared to question Authority and tradition.

In 2003 I attended a conference arranged by *Encounter*, an organization jointly set up by the British and Irish Governments. The conference was provocatively titled 'Post-Christian Society'. The majority of those invited to attend were Christians, and many began, predictably, by expressing the gravest of concerns about the current 'moral malaise'. The initial discussions were gloomy affairs that included much hand-wringing about the 'loss of values'.

But then the mood began to shift. Gradually, the delegates started to remind themselves that while things were, indeed, in some respects worse, they had, in others, undoubtedly improved. They began to remember just how dreadful were our moral attitudes to women, blacks and gays, for example. At the end of two days of discussions, the chairman asked those attending whether they thought that things were, morally speaking, better or worse than they were fifty years ago. Many of those present – my impression was the majority – while continuing to express concerns about a 'loss of values', nevertheless felt that, morally speaking, things were, on balance, *better* than they were half a century ago.

Yes we have, in some respects, rather *different* values now. And, in many cases, the right response to this is to say, 'And thank goodness for that.' Anyone who presents the changes in our moral values over the last half-century or so in an almost wholly bad light is guilty of grossly distorting the situation.

Bad Arguments for Relativism

Still, there are ways in which we are worse off, morally speaking. And it's arguable that these changes are in part a result of the rise of moral relativism. We saw at the end of the previous chapter how the spread of moral relativism is supposedly undermining the moral fabric of Western society. Moral relativism has supposedly become the dominant pop-philosophy of the age, and with disastrous consequences. So let's now turn our attention to relativism.

Let's now concede that the *Authoritarians are right about something.* They are right to reject moral relativism, certainly that crude form of non-judgementalist moral relativism that gets the blame for the 'moral malaise' (which is what, henceforth, we'll mean by 'relativism'). The usual, politically-motivated arguments for moral relativism and non-judgementalism are feeble, as I explain below.

As we saw in chapter six, relativists regularly point out that we Westerners have often arrogantly assumed we know best and that we have the right to force our own particular brand of morality down everyone else's throat. The Church has a particularly poor track record in this respect. We now acknowledge that we should be more open-minded and tolerant. We realize that we make mistakes. We know that there can often be a great deal to learn from other cultures. But doesn't recognizing all this require that we sign up to relativism?

Well, no, it doesn't. We can embrace all this good, liberal stuff without embracing moral relativism. Here are four key problems for relativism.

First of all, we can acknowledge that we're fallible about what's right and wrong, and that there can be much to learn from others, without accepting relativism. In fact, ironically, to acknowledge the possibility of our being mistaken requires that we *reject* relativism. For, if relativism is true, the truth about what's right and wrong depends on what we believe. If we believe so-and-so is wrong, then, for us, it is wrong. But then it turns out we can't be mistaken about what's right or wrong. It's relativism that makes us morally infallible. In order to acknowledge our own fallibility, we have to *reject* relativism.

Secondly, relativists can be notoriously *hypocritical*. The relativist who points a finger at the Westerner who judges female circumcision to be wrong and says 'It's wrong of you to judge!' ends up condemning themselves. For of course *they* are doing exactly what they are saying you shouldn't be doing. They are judging you, and saying that you're doing something morally wrong. Their politically-correct finger wagging is downright hypocritical.

Thirdly, politically-motivated moral relativists tend to apply their relativism pretty inconsistently. Take some remote and exotic rainforest tribe that engages in a practice most Westerners think barbaric and wrong. 'You shouldn't judge,' says the relativist. 'In their culture, this sort of behaviour is perfectly morally proper. And their morality is just as "valid" as yours.' But of course, if a large multi-national kicks out that tribe and hacks down that rainforest, the same relativist will no doubt be *most* judgemental. 'Stop. That's wrong,' they'll say. But of course they can't say that, can they? If they are going to be true to their relativism, then they must say that if the corporate culture deems it acceptable to destroy the rainforest and barbeque its inhabitants, then for them it *is* acceptable. Who are they to judge?

Finally, notice that it's only if we reject moral relativism that we are free to promote tolerance and open-mindedness as *universal* virtues. Take some religious culture that thinks it okay to be deeply intolerant. The relativist is going to have to say that, hey, if these religious zealots think it right to hack to death those with whom they disagree, then for them it *is* right: *who are we to judge?* Relativists can't consistently condemn the intolerance of others. It's only those who *reject* relativism that are free to do that.

So the usual, politically-motivated arguments for relativism really don't have much going for them. We can be good, right-on liberals with embracing relativism. Certainly, if you think we're morally fallible, and that tolerance is universally a virtue, you should reject this sort of relativism, not embrace it. At its worst, relativism turns out to be politically-correct twaddle of a rather noxious sort.

Liberals Who Reject Relativism

So let's agree with Authoritarian critics of Liberal education that relativism ought not to be encouraged. Let's enthusiastically reject relativism (certainly that brand of 'politically correct', non-judgementalist moral relativism on which the West's moral malaise is usually blamed). But then *many Liberals do*. While most of my friends and colleagues are pretty Liberal, I can't think of *any* who are moral relativists.

But here's the puzzle. One the one hand, many Liberals, myself included, reject relativism. Yet at the end of the previous chapter, we saw that many blame the moral malaise on relativism, which in turn gets blamed on the rise of Liberal attitudes. Liberals are repeatedly accused of spreading the cancer of moral relativism.

Clearly, someone is very confused. Is it we Liberals? Or is it our accusers?

Let's find out.

Eight

'Relativist!'

Before we look at the question of whether the Liberal approach to moral and religious education advocated in this book involves a commitment to moral relativism, let's set the scene by looking at how the charge of relativism is made more generally against 'liberals'.

The US has recently seen the publication of a number of books with titles like *How to Talk to a Liberal — If You Must* (Coulter 2004), *Persecution: How Liberals Are Waging War on Christianity* (Limbaugh 2003), and even *Help! Mom! There Are Liberals Under My Bed* (DeBrecht and Hummel 2005) (the publisher calls it 'the book conservative parents have been seeking'[1]). Some of these books accuse 'liberals' (whoever they are, exactly) of being stupid, amoral and unpatriotic. Some even suggest America is in the grip of a 'liberal' conspiracy to undermine Christianity and the American Way and turn your children gay.

Interestingly, among the various charges laid against 'liberals', relativism is one of the most popular. Let's take a look at a couple of examples.

In his inspiringly-titled *Let Freedom Ring*, Sean Hannity (2002: 137–138), political pundit at *Fox News*, suggests that one reason US 'liberals' are hostile to the teaching of the Declaration of Independence in public schools is that

... liberals absolutely abhor and militantly reject the Founders' belief in absolute truth. America's Founders believed deeply in certain fundamental truths about life, liberty, and the nature of man. In fact, they believed – they weren't just inserting lofty-sounding but meaningless platitudes in the document – that such truths were 'self-evident'. By sharp contrast, the Left embraces moral relativism with an arrogant tenacity.

There you are: 'liberals' – who, incidentally, Hannity seems to equate with 'the Left' – embrace moral relativism.

Limbaugh (2003), author of *Persecution: How Liberals Are Waging War Against Christianity*, also thinks 'liberals' are, or are mostly, relativists. Limbaugh responded in an interview to a comment about 'liberalism' by saying that while 'liberals'

> ... subscribe to moral relativism and no absolute truth, they betray their standards when it comes to judging Christians. They apply an absolute standard when it comes to Christians and they condemn us for our beliefs, so they're completely hypocritical on that. ... The Judeo-Christian ethic is one that is undergirded by absolute truth. Liberals, by and large, don't subscribe to any such value system (Interview by John Hawkins with Limbaugh on Limbaugh's book: *Persecution: How Liberals Are Waging War Against Christianity*).

Limbaugh here accuses 'liberals' of both relativism *and* hypocrisy: they proclaim relativism and non-judgementalism, yet here they are making moral judgements about Christian attitudes towards, say, homosexuality or the place of prayer in schools. Outrageous.

But are 'liberals', by and large, relativists?

Many people who describe themselves as 'liberal' reject relativism. Here in the UK, many call themselves 'liberal'. Among those I know, I'm not aware of any who consider themselves relativists. But maybe things are different in the US. Maybe, over the pond, 'liberals' do tend to sign up to the kind of hypocritical, non-judgementalist relativism of which they are repeatedly accused. But maybe not. Few of those who claim 'Liberals are relativists' appear to have done much research into the moral beliefs of those they describe as 'liberal'. Sometimes their evidence amounts to little more than a series of anecdotes. Undoubtedly, some 'liberals' do embrace moral relativism. Perhaps many do. But the suggestion that all, or most, of them are relativists seems poorly founded. Are most 'liberals' relativists? I have no idea. But then in many cases neither, I suspect, do those making the accusation.

And yet the factoid that 'liberals are relativists' has become heavily woven into the psyche of conservative America. Type 'liberal' and 'relativist' into Google and see what you get. I did, and quickly came up with a great deal of this sort of thing:

> The modern liberal is a self-proclaimed relativist, who does not
> believe in unbiased truth. Naturally, such a person does not
> believe in fairness or honesty either, both being relative.
> I do not say this is true of 100% of liberals, but it is true of
> most of them.[2]

On what evidence is this accusation made? None at all. In the US, the accusation 'Relativist' appears to have supplanted even 'Communist' in terms of its popularity, vitriol and baselessness.

Incidentally, another group endlessly dismissed as relativists are atheists (of whom there are comparatively few in the US). That all atheists are relativists is also a myth. Many of my friends and colleagues from both sides of the Atlantic are atheists. I'm not aware of any who are moral relativists (certainly not of the 'politically correct' variety). Nor does atheism entail relativism, as any good introduction to the philosophy of religion should explain (see, for example, 'Does Morality Depend On God And Religion?' in *The Philosophy Gym* (Law 2003)).

So that sets the scene: the charge of relativism is dished out repeatedly – in many cases without much foundation – by many on the political and religious right. It's an accusation they use to discredit their 'liberal' opponents.

Relativism and Liberalism-with-a-Capital-'L'

But what of Liberals-with-a-capital-'L'? What of the Liberal approach to moral education outlined in chapter three? Does *that* involve a commitment to moral relativism?

No. Liberals-with-a-capital-'L' needn't be relativists. There are similarities, of course. Both emphasize the importance of individual autonomy. But, as we'll see below, neither Liberalism, nor the Liberal approach to moral education advocated here, requires a commitment to relativism.

Science is Liberal, Not Relativist

Liberals recommend that individuals think critically and make their own judgement rather than more-or-less unquestioningly take on board the pronouncements of some external Authority. That does not require they embrace relativism and 'anything goes' non-judgementalism.

Compare empirical science. It too emphasizes the importance of independent critical thought. But to acknowledge the importance of getting scientists to think autonomously rather than uncritically defer to others is not to take the relativist view that all scientific theories – including even the theories that the sun goes round the Earth and that Mars is inhabited by giant wasps – are equally 'true'. It's not to say that science is just a matter of making up one's own scientific reality (as if, were we suddenly to change our minds about the Earth moving, it would immediately grind to a halt). Nor is it to embrace the non-judgementalist view that one scientist ought never to judge the theory of another. Obviously not, in fact.

Notice that, if this sort of scientific relativism were true, there would be no point to independent scientific investigation. Experiment and observation would be a waste of time. If every scientific opinion was as good as every other, then the judgement that a scientist arrived at after careful thought and study would be no better than the one they started with.

Clearly, to suggest that scientists ought to think independently rather than just uncritically defer to, say, the Authority of Aristotle or The Bible (as they tended to before the Enlightenment) is not to embrace relativism and non-judgementalism about scientific truth.

Exactly the same is true of morality. Indeed, it's precisely because proponents of the Liberal approach advocated here think there really is a non-relative truth to discover about what's right and what's wrong that they place so much emphasis on questioning and critical thinking. If we simply invent or make up morality, why bother being so scrupulously careful about *getting it right*? If every moral opinion is as good as every other, then the judgement I arrive at after much careful thought will be no better than the one I started with. If relativism were true, there would be *no point* bothering with the kind of critical thinking recommended here.

So the kind of Liberal approach outlined in chapter three is not committed to moral relativism. It is, in effect, opposed to it.

A Map of the Terrain

We can illustrate the point that Liberalism doesn't entail relativism by means of a diagram. We saw back in chapter two that the Liberal and Authoritarian positions lie on a scale. You can be more or less Liberal, and more or less Authoritarian, like so

Liberal ◀━━━━━━━━━━━━━━━━━━━▶ Authoritarian

This book recommends we situate ourselves well to the left on this scale.

Now the issue that divides moral relativists and non-relativists lies on another axis altogether, an axis that cuts across the Liberal/Authoritarian axis like so:

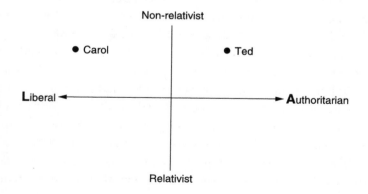

Meet Ted, a non-relativist and an Authoritarian. Ted is to be found in the top right hand corner of our diagram. Ted's position is a very traditional position, of course: the position of many religious conservatives. He believes there are objective, non-relative facts about right and wrong. Ted also believes that young people need to accept, more-or-less uncritically, these facts from those who know.

But non-relativists don't have to be Authoritarian. Take Carol, for example. Carol is in the top left corner. Carol agrees with Ted that there are absolute (i.e. non-relative) facts about right and wrong. She agrees that morality is certainly not a mere matter of subjective choice or preference. We can even suppose, if you like, that Carol is a Christian who believes that what's right and wrong has been objectively laid down by God. But still, Carol thinks each of us needs to figure out for ourselves what those facts are. Unlike Ted, Carol believes children should be taught and encouraged to think critically and independently. Carol rejects Ted's view that they should be told to defer more-or-less uncritically to Authority.

You can now see that there are more options available than just relativism (the bottom half of the chart) and Authoritarianism (the right hand side of the chart). To suppose that our choice is between relativism and Authoritarianism is to overlook the possibility of our occupying the top left hand corner of the chart. That's a corner Authoritarians tend to overlook. It's the corner I recommend we occupy.

A Philosophically Basic Point

None of this is rocket science, philosophically speaking. It's basic stuff. Philosophers regularly make the same point. Here, for example, is philosopher Le Poidevin (1996: 84–85) explaining it in characteristically clear fashion:

> To value moral autonomy is not ... to embrace moral scepticism and deny, or doubt, the existence of moral values. It is more likely to go together with an honest attempt to work out moral values ... Nor does autonomy necessarily lead one to moral relativism ...

The autonomous agent may well believe in the existence of objective moral values. Autonomy would then consist in working out what those values are.

But, despite being philosophically basic, it's a point lost on many critics of Liberal moral and religious education. They believe that *anyone who emphasizes the importance of moral autonomy must, by default, be a relativist.*

How a Liberal School Can *Combat* Relativism

Ironically, rather than being the root cause of relativism and non-judgementalism, a good Liberal education of the sort outlined in chapter three *can actually provide an effective defence against it.* A Liberal school can, and no doubt should, warn its pupils of the perils of moral relativism. Rather than promoting relativistic attitudes, *a Liberal school is free to explain, clearly and forcefully, exactly what's wrong with them.* If you want young people to reject moral relativism, is the best method to clamp down on independent, critical thought and insist they defer to external Authority? I suspect a more successful approach would be to give young people the skills they need to recognize for themselves exactly why the 'politically correct' arguments for relativism, while seductive, are muddle-headed nonsense.

Religious Education and Relativism

What's also ironic, given the tendency of religious Authoritarians to blame Liberals for the rise of relativism, is that one of its causes may yet turn out to be the *desire not to challenge religious Authority.*

Many schools now teach children about a range of religions (in many cases they are required to). This can put teachers in a difficult position. Religions make claims that are incompatible. Christians believe Jesus is God[3] and also that he was physically resurrected. Muslims, on the other hand, deny both these claims. For Muslims, Jesus is no more than an important prophet.

Now some children, when presented with these conflicting belief systems, will inevitably ask, 'But which is actually *true?* Which religion actually gets things right?' That's a shrewd question, and, if you're a teacher, a potentially awkward one, particularly if you want to avoid undermining religious Authority. Admit to little Mary that it does indeed look as if at least one of these two religions must be false, and she may rush home and tell her devoutly Catholic parents she's being taught that the Christian religion may be false and the Pope might be mistaken. Phone calls may ensue.

So some teachers reach for relativism to get them off the hook. They say, 'Er ... well, both religions are right. That Jesus is God is true-for-Christians but false-for-Muslims.' Relativism saves educators from having to admit that any religion might actually be mistaken, or even (heaven forbid) that they might all be mistaken. Far safer to wheel out relativism, on which they're all correct.

Marilyn Mason, education officer at the British Humanist Association, has noticed this trend. She suggests that it is, ironically, *religious education (RE) itself that has largely been responsible for the spread of relativistic attitudes among the young.* The cure, she thinks, is a rather more philosophical approach, with the emphasis on clear, critical thinking.

> I used to wonder where my students' shoulder shrugging relativism and subjectivism about knowledge came from, though I think I now know: talk of 'different truths' or 'subjective truth' seems to have become the accepted RE way of demonstrating tolerance and mutual respect when confronted with differing and sometimes conflicting beliefs and views on morality or the supernatural ... Here is an area where the clear thinking characteristic of philosophy at its best would surely help (Mason 2005: 37).

A more philosophically rigorous approach to religious education would certainly help weed out the flabby evasion 'That's true-for-Christians but false-for-Muslims'.[4]

Relativist vs Liberal Responses to Home-Grown Religious Fanaticism

Here's another illustration of how modern day Liberals are assumed to be relativists. As we saw in chapter seven, relativism faces a difficulty when it comes to promoting tolerance as a *universal* virtue.

It seems that, when faced with the violent intolerance of others, the relativist must say, 'Hey – if that's what they believe, *then they're right*. Who are we to judge?'

But this leaves a relativist society defenceless against, say, intolerant religious fanatics that spring up within their own midst. This point is often made. In *The End of History and the Last Man*, Fukuyama (1992: 328) writes that

> [r]elativism – the doctrine that all values are merely relative ... must ultimately end up undermining democratic and tolerant values ... It fires indiscriminately, shooting out the legs of not only the 'absolutisms', dogmas, and certainties of the western tradition, but that tradition's emphasis on tolerance, diversity and freedom of thought as well.

Faced with intolerant religious zealots, the relativist has to say, 'If these guys believe liberal democracy, tolerance and freedom of thought are a menace that must be wiped from the face of the Earth, then they're right. We must stand back and let them get on with it. After all, who are we to judge?' Fukuyama (1992: 332) concludes that:

> Modern thought raises no barriers to a future nihilistic war against liberal democracy on the part of those brought up within its bosom.

But Fukuyama's final conclusion is false. Relativism may be defence-less against home-grown illiberal, religious fanatics. Liberalism with a capital 'L' is not. Liberals are free to combat intolerance and fight for freedom of speech, as we saw back in chapter five. There's no inconsistency or hypocrisy involved in Liberals battling this sort of zealotry. As 'modern thought' clearly contains within it a strong Enlightened, Liberal, non-relativist tradition, *Fukuyama is mistaken when he claims it lacks the resources to deal with this internal threat*. Here's an illustration of how even sophisticated social commentators like Fukuyama can end up overlooking the non-relativist Liberal point of view.

The 'Culture War'

So the kind of Liberal moral and religious education advocated here is not relativist. Nor does it entail or promote relativism. Quite the opposite, in fact. Indeed, it provides us with a powerful tool with which to *combat* relativism. And yet *the myth that a Liberal moral education must promote relativism is unfortunately a myth for which a great many Authoritarians have fallen.*

One way in which the myth manifests itself is in talk of a 'culture war'. In the minds of many, the West is currently engaged in a kind of civil war – a war of ideas and values. On one side are arrayed the relativists, who think all moral points of view are equally 'true' and that consequently 'anything goes'. On the other side are the defenders of traditional values.

Those who talk of a 'culture war' typically see themselves as the defenders of the underdogs – those sensible men and women who stick by their solid, Bible-based values – against the 'liberal elite' with their fancy relativist ideas. Take the US Christian fundamentalist Pat Buchanan, who writes that

> America is locked in a cultural war for the soul of our country. On one side: secularists armed with the proposition that God is dead. They preach a hedonistic dogma where man is the highest authority and his whim is the only absolute. They claim that God's law has no place in our courtrooms, and his name no place in our classrooms. Their governing axioms reduce faith to superstition and traditional morality to quaint nonsense. No fixed standards of right and wrong, beautiful or debased, healthy or sick. If it feels good, do it ... The mob listened, and today, we reap relativism's poisoned harvest.[5]

Not everyone who speaks of a 'culture war' is quite as blunt as Buchanan. Himmelfarb (1999), for example, author of *One Nation, Two Cultures*, presents a rather more nuanced version of the theory. But the gist is essentially the same – you're either with the God-fearing moral traditionalists, or else you're with the relativistic, morally degenerate 'liberal elite'.

So prevalent has this idea of a culture war become in the US that moral traditionalists can now buy guides on how to engage in intellectual trench warfare with the enemy. Kreeft's *How to Win the Culture War* is a popular example that 'maps out key battlefields', 'issues a strategy for engagement' and 'equips Christians with the weapons needed for a successful campaign' (2002: back cover).

While the idea that the West is experiencing a culture war is not yet commonplace in the UK, its popularity is growing. Phillips (1998) has certainly embraced the concept. She writes that 'Britain is in the grip of a culture war' between defenders of 'external authority' like herself, and the relativists on the other (Phillips 1998: 65). We are, she claims, experiencing 'nothing less than a culture war between two opposing mindsets' (Phillips 1998: xxix).

This culture war is also, of course, a war for children's minds, and moral and religious education is at the front line. As proponents of the culture war theory see it, their mission is to rescue the next generation from the poisonous relativism of the 'liberal elite' and reground children in traditional values.

The Relativism-or-Authoritarianism Myth

So where would a culture war theorist place a proponent of the sort of Liberal, philosophical approach to moral and religious education outlined in chapter three? Remember, my sort of Liberal has no problem with the teaching of, say, traditional Judeo-Christian moral values. And I too reject relativism. So you might think that a Liberal like myself would receive a warm welcome in Himmelfarb and Phillips' army. Perhaps Buchanan will want to sign me up as a new recruit.

But of course Liberals-with-a-capital-'L' are not welcome. Indeed, those who speak of a 'culture war' typically perceive Liberals to be the enemy. They don't just want Judeo-Christian values taught, they want the emphasis placed on traditional, Authority-based moral and religious teaching. As far as they are concerned, the Liberal approach, with its emphasis on moral autonomy, involves a commitment to relativism. Anyone who rejects religious Authority is therefore immediately assumed to be a relativist. And so, as these 'culture war' theorists see it, our choice is simple: *return to religious Authority and achieve salvation or stick with the prevailing relativism and slide into moral oblivion.*

How Relativists Caricature Liberals

Actually, it's not just Authoritarians who tend to argue that our choice is between Authority and relativism. Relativists have, in effect, fallen for the very same 'culture war' myth. But while Authoritarians tend to assume Liberals are relativists, relativists often make the reverse mistake: *they assume Liberals must be Authoritarians.*

Back in the 1970s, when relativism was much more in the ascendant, it was indeed the relativists who most obviously fell for the Authoritarianism-or-relativism myth. They would assume any opponent of relativism must be an Authoritarian, and therefore Bad News. 'This person *says* he wants children to think for themselves,' they would say, 'but the truth is he simply wants to ram his own white, male reactionary views down children's throats under the pretext that this is what "reason" demands. He really just wants to exert *power* over young minds. He's a jackbooted bully intent on brainwashing our children into accepting what *he* decrees is true. If you reject Authoritarianism, as any tolerant right-thinking liberal must, then you should side with us relativists against Authoritarians like him.'

This is also hogwash. The approach set out in chapter three is not to get young people uncritically to accept whatever we tell them. The idea is to get them to apply their own powers of reason and make their own judgements. Critical thinking is not some sinister form of thought-control – in fact it's one of the best defences *against* thought-control. And yet, by accusing all Liberals of being Authoritarians, some relativists had considerable success in convincing people that that it is what Liberals are. In their confusion, they foisted a false dilemma on the public: 'You're either a nasty Authoritarian like him, or you're a cuddly, tolerant relativist like us.' Understandably, presented with just those options, some sided with the relativists.

The Great Myth

So, in my view, many relativists and Authoritarians are guilty of falling for the same basic myth: that we must choose between them. This myth continues to dominate moral debate. In particular, listen to a radio or TV discussion on some topical moral issue and you'll find that anyone who rejects the conservative, religious position is likely sweepingly to be dismissed as a relativist.

During the 1960s and 1970s, moral relativism became increasingly fashionable. Now the pendulum is swinging back in the direction of Authority, with ever more panicky warnings of moral meltdown if we don't reject relativism and root the child's moral education in some external religious Authority. We seem forced to choose between two equally repugnant, and equally dangerous, positions: relativism or Authoritarianism. Either that or accept some bizarre combination of the two.

The central message of this book is this: rather than ping-ponging back and forth between relativism and Authoritarianism, we should acknowledge that these are not the only options. By being both Liberal and non-relativist, we can avoid the dangers of both Authoritarianism and relativism.

It's time we finally nailed the relativism-or-Authoritarianism myth — a myth that has, for decades, dangerously distorted the whole 'morality debate'. In particular, it's high time that Liberals started challenging, vigorously, those who continue to fall for it. Which is how I intend to tie up this chapter. Let's finish with three cases studies — three typical examples of how Liberals are assumed to be relativists.

Case Study 1: www.moral-relativism.com

The first example comes from www.moral-relativism.com, a US website dedicated to combating moral relativism and promoting Christian values. In the following quotation, the author helpfully begins by outlining what moral relativism is, before accusing the

President of the Planned Parenthood Federation of America (PPFA) of being a relativist.

> Moral relativism has steadily been accepted as the primary moral philosophy of modern society, a culture that was previously governed by a 'Judeo-Christian' view of morality. ... [M]ost people hold to the concept that right or wrong are not absolutes, but can be determined by each individual. Morals and ethics can be altered from one situation, person, or circumstance to the next. Essentially, moral relativism says that anything goes ... Words like 'ought' and 'should' are rendered meaningless. In this way, moral relativism makes the claim that it is morally neutral.
> In describing her view on morality, the President of Planned Parenthood Federation of America once stated, '... teaching morality doesn't mean imposing my moral values on others. It means sharing wisdom, giving reasons for believing as I do – and then trusting others to think and judge for themselves.'
> She claims to be morally neutral, yet her message is clearly intended to influence the thinking of others ... an intention that is not, in fact, neutral (www.moral-relativism.com).

The author thinks the President of the PPFA is inconsistent. The President is a relativist who thinks all opinions are equally good, yet she goes round promoting her own opinion as the right one. What blatant hypocrisy.

But take a closer look at what the President of the PPFA actually says. Does she say she favours moral relativism? No. She merely says that she doesn't want to 'impose' her views on others. But she does want to give her views, and explain why she holds them. She is happy to defend them. But she also wants students to 'think and judge for themselves'. That's a very Liberal view. The President of the PPFA does not commit herself to relativism. There's nothing inconsistent about a Liberal wanting to influence young people by means of rational persuasion and open debate.

All this is entirely lost on the author of the above attack, however, who, having spotted the President of the PPFA is a Liberal, immediately weighs in with a witch-finder's shriek of 'Relativist!'.

Case Study 2: Melanie Phillips' Attack on Graham Haydon

The author and columnist Melanie Phillips has, on a number of occasions, conflated Liberalism and relativism. In her book *All Must Have Prizes*, Phillips (1996: 220) claims that the Enlightenment emphasis on raising morally autonomous individuals results in a teaching culture of non-judgementalism, in which all moral points must be deemed equally valid, effectively 'destroying the teacher's ability to teach right from wrong' and undermining discipline because 'rules are taboo' (p. 28).

But of course a Liberal, Enlightened approach to moral education does *not* require teachers to be non-judgemental and abandon rules and discipline. We nailed those confusions back in chapter two.

A typical example of how Phillips confuses Liberalism and relativism crops up in her attack on the philosopher of education Graham Haydon. Phillips quotes a passage in which Haydon warns of the perils of getting children to adopt an attitude of deference to Authority and tradition. Here's what Haydon actually says.

> It still must be said forcefully that accepting uncritically what someone tells you because they are seen to be in authority is not a good thing ... Doing what is right cannot be a matter of doing what one is told. Schools must produce people who are able to think for themselves what is right ... It will not take an exceptionally clever pupil, or an exceptionally bolshie one, to ask: 'How do we know this is right or that is wrong?' Any pupil who is being taught to think ought to be asking such questions. And the same pupil ought to see that 'Because I say so' is not an acceptable answer. Nor is 'because these are the values of your society'. When exposed to a little more teaching of history, perhaps, this pupil will see that by such an argument the value of slave states and Nazi states would have to be endorsed (Phillips 1996: 221–222).

Haydon's position as sketched out above is clearly Liberal. But Phillips considers Haydon's argument 'dangerous'. Haydon is setting his pupils on the road to 'despotism and tyranny' (Phillips 1996: 222).

Why? Because, says Phillips, Haydon is *promoting moral relativism*. He's encouraging his pupils to think that there are no facts about what is right and what is wrong – it's all just a matter of subjective taste or opinion.

> Haydon's attitude opened the way for his pupils to say that racial prejudice was no less right than tolerance; or that it was permissible to kill people because they were genetically imperfect. Moral relativism leads directly to despotism and tyranny (Phillips 1996: 222).

But where in the above-quoted paragraph does Haydon commit himself to moral relativism? Where does he espouse non-judgementalism? Nowhere. Haydon is just as free as Phillips to argue forcefully *against* relativism. He's merely recommending that his pupils think independently, rather than accept uncritically the judgement of Authority. That's not to sign up to relativism.

In her haste to attack Haydon, Phillips misses this philosophically basic point.[6]

Case Study 3: Sacks' Attack on Kant

In a recent book, Jonathan Sacks, the UK's Chief Rabbi, also muddles up Liberalism and relativism. Like Phillips, Sacks lays the blame for our moral malaise firmly at the feet of the Enlightenment, and particularly at the feet of Kant, about whom we have already seen that Sacks writes,

> [A]ccording to Kant ... [t]o do something because others do, or because of habit or custom or even Divine Command, is to accept an external authority over the one sovereign territory that is truly our own: our own choices. The moral being for Kant is by definition an autonomous being, a person who accepts no other authority than the self. By the 1960s this was beginning to gain hold as an educational orthodoxy. The task of education is not to hand on a tradition but to enhance the consciousness of choice (Sacks 1997: 176).

Sacks is correct that Kant is an arch-Liberal who insists that individuals should judge for themselves rather than defer to external Authority. We saw back in chapter five that Kant appears to be right – the responsibility to judge has a boomerang-like quality. In the end, it does always come back to you – the individual. Yet Sacks rejects this Kantian emphasis on the moral autonomy of the individual. In particular, says Sacks, a Kantian approach to moral education requires *non-judgementalism and relativism on the part of the teacher*' (Sacks 1997: 176).

No it doesn't. To insist that individuals be educated to make their own judgement is not to insist that all judgements are equally 'true'. As should now be clear, Sacks' point is rather badly muddled.

Incidentally, there's another way in which Sacks gives Kant's thinking a relativistic twist. The dubious word is 'choice'.

Although you might not have guessed it from the above quotation, Kant's view is *not* that what is right and wrong is a matter of 'choice'. According to Kant, right and wrong are established by reason. But that's not to say Kant thinks that any conclusion you might draw is as good as any other. If you apply your powers of reason and come to the conclusion that killing is morally acceptable, then you have made a mistake, just as surely as someone who calculates that 12 times 12 is 145 has made a mistake. You can no more 'choose' that killing is morally permissible than you can 'choose' that 12 times 12 comes to 145. Kant doesn't think we are 'autonomous' in the sense that the answer to a moral question is whatever we *choose* it to be. Kant doesn't suppose we each get to *make up* our own morality to suit ourselves.

By including the word 'choice' in his characterization, Sacks gives the impression that Kant thinks morality boils down to nothing more than subjective preference. Again, that's a (no doubt unintentional) caricature.

Conclusion

One popular objection to the kind of Liberal approach to moral and religious education advocated in this book is that it promotes moral relativism, which in turn undermines the moral fabric of society. If we want to repair the damage relativism has done, we must return to more traditional, Authority-based methods of morally educating young people.

In this chapter, we've seen why this attack on Liberal education fails miserably. The kind of Liberal approach recommended here is profoundly *opposed to* relativism. In truth, it's particularly well-placed to *combat* the shoddy 'That's-true-for-us but false-for-them' brand of relativism that you come across in some classrooms.

The central argument of this chapter is that it's important we no longer fall for the myth that our options are either moral relativism or a return to traditional religious-Authority-based values education. It's particularly important that defenders of Authority are no longer allowed sweepingly to dismiss their Liberal opponents as relativists. This misconception needs to be challenged. Forcefully.

True, the myths tackled in this chapter are, from the point of view of most academics, rather silly myths. Some may wonder why I'm even bothering to tackle the various religious leaders, journalists and other social commentators that have fallen for them. The reason is that these popular commentators have been very successful in shaping public opinion. Because they've been allowed endlessly to repeat this anti-Enlightenment mythology without ever being effectively publicly challenged, they are beginning to influence the prevailing zeitgeist. They are starting to drive public opinion back in the direction of Authority.

One final point: those who wave a hand in the direction of the moral malaise and say 'But look at the awful results of your Liberal approach. Look at the moral malaise which Liberal educational methods have produced' are also rather overlooking the fact that the approach advocated here has actually only ever been tested in a handful of schools. In which case it can hardly be to blame for the moral malaise. Perhaps *some* forms of Liberal moral education (i.e. 'hands off', relativistic, non-judgemental forms of moral education) are to blame for our current moral difficulties. But of course that's not the kind of education recommended in this book. Discrediting *that* sort of 'Liberal' moral education does nothing to discredit the Liberal approach advocated here.

Nine

The War for Children's Minds

Let's now turn to a different attack on Liberal moral and religious education.

This book argues that, when it comes to judgements about right and wrong, it's a mistake to encourage children and young adults to accept uncritically the pronouncements of some external authority. They should be encouraged and trained to think for themselves. But isn't this vastly to overestimate what an individual, armed only with their power of reason, can do? Is it possible for an individual, just by applying their own rationality, to figure out what's right and wrong? The answer to that, many would say, is 'no'. An individual, left with nothing but the power of their own intellect, is left stranded, like a frog at the bottom of a well, unable to attain any moral bearings at all. Reason alone is morally blind. Someone who thinks that stealing is morally acceptable need not be any less *rational* than someone selflessly devoted to helping others. Their mistake is not one of logic. But *if morality is not ultimately a matter of reason, isn't it a mistake to place so much emphasis on it?* If my power of reason is ultimately incapable of distinguishing right from wrong, *surely I have no choice but to place my faith in some external Authority that can supply that moral knowledge for me?*

There may be something right in this objection. But there's a great deal wrong with it. Before we identify exactly what is wrong with it, let's briefly sketch out one (though not the only) line of argument that might seem to support the conclusion that morality has ultimately got little if anything to do with reason.

The argument is, in essence, that of the Eighteenth Century philosopher David Hume (1739: book 2, part 3, section III).

Truths of Reason

One way in which the rabbit of morality could be conjured out of the hat of reason would be if moral truths were, or could be reduced to, logical truths. Consider the claim:

> All triangles have three sides.

You can establish that this claim is true just by thinking about it. Triangles are, by definition, three-sided. So someone who claims that there exists a triangle lacking three sides has, in effect, contradicted themselves: the triangle in question would have to be both three-sided and not three-sided. That triangles have three sides is, in this sense, a logical truth.

Might moral truths similarly turn out to be logical truths? It seems not. Someone who claims that, say, stealing isn't wrong hasn't contradicted themselves. While we possess a logical guarantee that all triangles have three sides, we possess no such guarantee when it comes to the wrongness of stealing.

Still, even if the claim that stealing is wrong is not a logical truth, perhaps logic still might be used to justify it. Perhaps it might be justified by means of a sound argument. Let's start by clarifying what sound argument involves.

The Sausage Machine of Reason

The wonderful thing about a sound argument is its power to preserve truth. Take the following argument, for example.

1. Frank is a man.
2. All men live on the Earth.
Conclusion: Frank lives on the Earth.

This argument takes the form of two claims, or premises, and a conclusion. In a deductive argument, like this one, the premises are supposed logically to entail the conclusion. The argument, if valid, provides us with a logical guarantee: if the premises are true, then so is the conclusion. In this case, the argument is valid. The premises really do entail the conclusion.

Of course, if you feed one or more falsehoods into a valid deductive argument, then there's no guarantee what you will get. The conclusion might still be true. But it might be false. (Suppose, for example, that the first premise of our argument is false: Frank isn't a man – he's an alien living on the planet Pluto; then our conclusion isn't true.)

So a valid deductive argument is truth-preserving. If you have fed true premises in, then you're logically guaranteed to get a true conclusion out. If you're interested in believing things that are actually true, this is a nice result.

For those who like analogies, we might say that valid forms of deductive argument function a bit like a sausage machine. Only, instead of feeding sausage meat in and getting sausages out the other side, it's guaranteed that if we feed true premises in, we'll get true conclusions out.

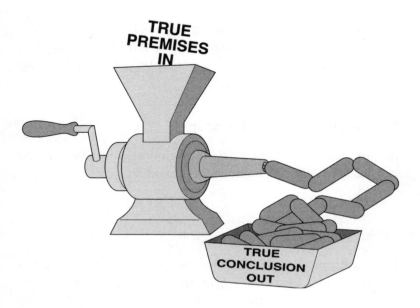

The Inductive Sausage Machine

Deductive argument isn't the only sound form of argument. There's also *inductive* reasoning. Here's an example of an inductive argument:

1. Apple one contains pips.
2. Apple two contains pips.
3. Apple three contains pips.
[...]
1000. Apple one thousand contains pips.
Conclusion: All apples contain pips.

This argument has one thousand premises (though I have only bothered to list four of them). In an inductive argument the premises are supposed to support the conclusion.[1] The key word here is *support*. Clearly, this argument is not (and isn't meant to be) deductively valid. The premises do not deductively entail the conclusion. There's no logical guarantee that the next apple won't have pips, no matter how many apples with pips we've examined up to now. But still, we suppose that the fact that every apple we have examined up to now has contained pips makes it *pretty reasonable* for us to conclude they all do.[2] The premises, we suppose, make the truth of the conclusion fairly likely. If that's right, then sound inductive arguments also have a truth-preserving, sausage-machine-like quality. Feed true premises into a sound inductive argument, and you're *likely* to get a true conclusion out the other end.

Again, if the truth is what you are after, that's a nice result.

Hume and the Is/Ought Gap

We have seen that sound argument tends to be truth-preserving. That's why a sound argument with true premises is able to *justify* a conclusion — such as argument can show that the conclusion is, or is probably, true.

So how might we use sound argument to justify a moral conclusion? Let's start by distinguishing *two different sorts of premise* upon which our reasoning might be based.

The philosopher David Hume famously distinguished 'is' claims and 'ought' claims. Science is fundamentally concerned with establishing how the world *is*. Scientists *observe* what is the case, of course. They note that these different samples of water all boiled at 100°C, that the sun rose yesterday and today, and so on. They also *theorize* about what is the case. They claim, for example, that *all* water boils at 100°C – even the water they haven't tested yet.

Morality, on the other hand, appears to deal with an entirely different category of claim. Morality does not describe how the world *is*. It says how it *ought* to be. Take, for example, the claim that *stealing is wrong*. Superficially, this looks like an 'is' claim (it contains the word 'is'). But actually, on closer examination, it seems not to make a claim about how things are. Certainly, to claim that stealing is wrong is not, for example, to claim that anyone *is* or *isn't* stealing anything. It's to claim only that we *ought not* to steal.

Now if we want to use deductive or inductive reasoning to support a moral conclusion – an 'ought' conclusion – what sort of premise must we feed in? Can we, for instance, generate 'ought' conclusions by feeding in 'is' claims?

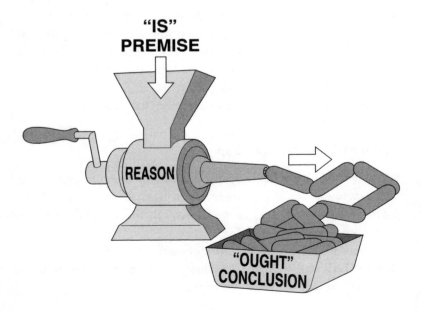

Hume, famously, denies this. He argues that claims about what is the case are morally neutral. They won't allow us to draw any conclusions about what we ought or ought not to do.

Take, for example, mugging old ladies. That's something almost everyone agrees we ought not to do. But why? Obviously, mugging old ladies makes them miserable. It may result in their physical harm or death. It results in anxiety for their friends, family and also the wider community. Doesn't that immediately rationally justify us in concluding we ought not to do it?

No, says Hume. After all, the psychopath who thinks that mugging old ladies is something we ought to go in for can be in complete agreement about all these 'is' facts. 'Yes,' he'll say, 'mugging old ladies causes them great misery and worse. But hey, that's exactly why I do it! I think that is something we *ought* to do.' This response may strike us as very weird indeed. But is this person being irrational? It seems not. The psychopath agrees with us about the 'is' claim:

Mugging old ladies causes them great misery (etc.).

And our conclusion

We *ought not* to mug old ladies

is no more deductively or inductively supported by that 'is' claim than is the psychopath's belief:

We *ought* to mug old ladies.

There appears to be, as philosophers like to put it, an *is/ought gap* – it seems that claims about what *is* the case fail to provide any rational support to conclusions about what we *ought* or *ought not* to do.[3]

The Circularity Problem

So how, then, might we use our 'sausage machine' to justify our moral conclusions? It seems that the only way we are going to get an 'ought' conclusion out is if we feed at least one 'ought' premise in.

Here's a simple example:

1. You *ought* always to repay a debt.
2. You owe Ted one pound.
Conclusion: You *ought* to repay Ted the one pound you owe him.

This little argument is cogent. It's an example of the kind of simple reasoning we might use to spell out to a child why they ought to pay back that pound they owe. But of course, while the argument is sound, it takes for granted a moral premise. We have succeeded in squeezing out an 'ought' conclusion only because we helped ourselves to at least one 'ought' premise. And how, you might wonder, is *that* premise to be justified?

You can see the general difficulty. While we might use reason to justify one moral claim by means of another (e.g. we might justify one moral principle by appealing to another more basic one), there's a problem when it comes to justifying our *entire* moral position, including our most basic moral beliefs. For then we no longer have any 'oughts' to feed in other than those we are trying to justify. And of course we can't use our moral beliefs to justify themselves. A circular justification is no justification at all. After all, if *that* were an acceptable way to justify a set of moral beliefs, then the psychopath could just as effectively use it to justify his own twisted sense of right and wrong.

So where does that leave us, so far as using reason to justify our moral beliefs is concerned? In deep trouble, it seems.

The conclusion some now draw is: *reason is quite incapable of justifying our overall moral stance on life.* It can't rationally support one consistent set of basic moral beliefs over another. The belief system of a psychopath may, in truth, be no more or less *rational* or *reasonable* than that of a saint. Hume (1739) concludes that the principles of morality are not the product of reason.

> It is not contrary to reason to prefer the destruction of the whole world to the scratching of my finger.

Now my intention is not to endorse the Humean argument sketched out above. It has its flaws.[4] The argument is presented merely as an illustration and to prepare the ground for the argument that follows.

But still, let's suppose, if only for the sake of argument, that Hume's conclusion is correct. What are the repercussions of this for the Liberal approach outlined in chapter three?

First, some may conclude that if morality cannot be given a rational foundation, then it must be a mistake to emphasize, as this book does, the importance of getting individuals to apply their own powers of reason to moral questions. Secondly, some may go further and conclude that if morality cannot ultimately be rooted in reason, then it will *have* to be rooted in some external Authority, such as a religious text or leader, instead.

Defending the Liberal Approach

But in fact neither of those two conclusions follow. This book defends the view that individuals ought to be encouraged to think and judge for themselves about right and wrong. But notice, first of all, that this is not to take any particular view about where moral points of view *originate*.

Of course, most of our moral beliefs do not originate in reason. Many people derive at least some of their moral beliefs from their religion. Some get them from their parents. Some take them from their community. Occasionally they are drawn from some sort of religious experience. Some of our moral beliefs may even be innate – hard-wired into us by natural selection (which would explain why we tend to find ourselves 'stuck' with more or less the same beliefs, whatever our background).[5] The concern here is not to defend any particular theory about where our moral beliefs do, or should, come from. The concern is to defend a view about the kind of attitude we should foster in individuals towards these beliefs, wherever they originate.

Should individuals be encouraged to accept more or less uncritically the moral beliefs handed down to them by their religion, their community, their genes, or the voice of God in their head? The view defended here is that, wherever your moral beliefs happen to come from, you should be encouraged to think critically about them. Pointing out that morality does not, indeed *cannot*, originate in reason leaves this point unscathed.

Some will question this. They may ask, 'If Hume is correct and reason is wholly incapable of justifying our most basic moral principles, then what on earth is the point of applying reason to moral questions? Surely we want individuals to believe what is true. And you have, in effect, just conceded that, when it comes to right and wrong, reason is wholly incapable of helping us arrive at the truth.'

But we have conceded no such thing. Reason alone may be incapable of determining right and wrong, but that is not to say that establishing what is right and wrong has nothing to do with reason. It still has a great deal to do with it. Thinking carefully and critically about your moral beliefs may be highly revealing. Here are four examples of how reason can still be constructively applied.

1. Revealing Unacknowledged Consequences

First, a little critical analysis may reveal unacknowledged *consequences* of your existing moral beliefs.

Suppose, for example, that you believe we ought not to discriminate against others unless there is some relevant reason to do so. Yes, adults discriminate against children – they prevent them from driving cars, voting and so on – but adults are justified in discriminating in this way because there is a *morally relevant difference* between us and them – children are not yet sufficiently smart or responsible to drive or vote. When it comes to denying women or black people the vote on the other hand, there is no morally relevant difference. Black people and women are different to white males of course, and in obvious ways. But differences in sexual organs or skin-colour are not relevant when it comes to justifying withholding the right to vote. That's why it is wrong to discriminate in this way. Those who do so are guilty of bigotry.

This principle of non-discrimination is, on the face of it, highly plausible. Almost all of us are willing to sign up to something like it. But few of us have thought through its full consequences.

Take for example other species – pigs, dogs, cows, etc. We discriminate against them too, and fairly dramatically at that. We experiment on them, and kill and eat them. Yet we think it would be wrong to treat any human in that way. Now, given our principle, if this discrimination is not also to qualify as bigotry, we need to come up with some *morally relevant difference* between humans and other species that justifies this difference in treatment. And that is notoriously difficult to do.

For example, some say: 'Well, other species are less sophisticated and intelligent than us. *That's* why it is okay to kill and eat them.' But this justification would also justify us in killing and eating mentally impaired human beings – something almost everyone considers shockingly immoral. It's hard to explain why the way in which we discriminate between humans and other species doesn't involve a form of bigotry akin to racism or sexism.

Now my aim isn't to defend this charge of bigotry. I use this example merely to illustrate the point that, by applying our powers of reason and thinking through the consequences of our moral convictions, we *may* discover surprising consequences. We may discover that what we thought was morally acceptable is actually not morally acceptable at all.

So here is one important role that reason can play in revealing what is morally true. By feeding an agreed 'ought' premise (in this case, concerning discrimination) into our 'sausage machine', we may be able to uncover *unrecognized consequences*.

2. Revealing Logical Inconsistencies

The application of reason may also reveal *inconsistencies* within our system of moral beliefs, requiring us to change at least some of them. The beliefs we might come under rational pressure to change may even include some of our most trenchantly held moral convictions.

Suppose, for example, that I have a profound commitment both to the principle that human life is intrinsically more valuable than any other form of life, and also to the principle of non-discrimination outlined above. On thinking through the consequences of the latter principle, I might eventually find that I hold a logically inconsistent moral position. I may find reason places me under intolerable pressure to give up at least one of these two deeply held convictions.

Indeed, some of mankind's greatest moral breakthroughs have come about, at least in part, through just such critical thought. Those who fought hardest both for the abolition of slavery and for the emancipation of women included many motivated by their religious convictions. But what set these individuals apart and made such radical movers and shakers was their willingness to question the prevailing wisdom of the time, to work through, clearly and rigorously, the consequences of their most basic moral beliefs. They had the courage to question the orthodox religious views of the day. They followed Kant's advice and *dared to think*. By so doing, they embodied precisely the kind of Enlightenment-inspired attitude to morality advocated here.[6]

3. The Role of Scientific Reasoning

Despite the is/ought gap, science still has a role to play when it comes to figuring out what's right and what's wrong. Take, for example, the moral issues surrounding embryo and stem cell research. Science alone cannot tell us whether we should allow it. But it can still help us arrive at the right decision. If, for example, we believe that what qualifies something for moral consideration is the ability to feel pain, then a scientific investigation into whether embryos have nervous systems, and if so, just how developed those systems are, suddenly becomes very pertinent.

Indeed, moral disagreements are often *partly* factual. The dispute over whether or not women should be allowed the vote was, in part, a dispute over whether women have the necessary intellectual skills to exercise that right properly. That they do is a matter of empirically demonstrable fact.

So by combining scientific discoveries about what is the case with agreed 'ought' premises, we may still use our sausage machine to derive important moral conclusions – about, for example, women's suffrage or stem cell research.

4. Revealing Faulty Reasoning

Reason can also reveal where someone's moral position is dependent on faulty argument. By thinking carefully and critically, we may reveal where others, and we ourselves, may have slipped up in drawing moral conclusions. Spotting these slips can be crucially important.

Take, for example, someone who attempts to justify the moral condemnation of homosexuals on the grounds that homosexuality is 'unnatural'. In this case, their reasoning is faulty precisely because it falls foul of Hume's is/ought gap: the premise that homosexuality is unnatural no more rationally supports the conclusion that it *ought not* to be practised than it does the conclusion that it *ought* to be practised. Even if homosexuality were, as a matter of fact, 'unnatural' (which it probably isn't), that would not, by itself, justify us in morally condemning it.[7]

To sum up, while science and reason may not be able to justify our most basic moral principles, they can still have far-reaching ramifications once certain principles have been agreed. They can also make us see why those principles ought to be revised.

Someone who is unwilling or unable to think carefully and critically about their moral beliefs is therefore at a serious disadvantage, morally speaking. Their inability to see the inconsistencies, fallacies and false presuppositions in their own thinking makes them far more susceptible to condoning, or even engaging in, the morally indefensible – such as slavery, sexism or the persecution of Jews and homosexuals.

A Final Worry

Here's a final worry that might still be raised about the emphasis this book places on reason. Someone may say,

> Suppose Kant is mistaken and reason cannot underpin morality. Then, by insisting that individuals 'think for themselves', you're making them rely on their own subjective feelings instead. Moral judgements will ultimately have to be made on the basis

of whatever 'feels right' to each individual. But this is far too subjective, and is likely to lead to individuals making moral judgements that are essentially shallow and self-serving. You are ultimately bringing morality down to subjective preference or choice – to 'I want' and 'I feel' rather than 'I ought'. Better that individuals rely on an external moral Authority that can provide them with an objective moral yardstick.

This move is superficially appealing. But on closer examination it's fatally flawed.

First (and this is probably the most devastating objection), even if it's conceded that reason cannot underpin morality, that doesn't immediately give us a reason for favouring an external-Authority-based approach to moral education over a Liberal one. For if individuals defer to some external moral Authority, and that Authority cannot rationally underpin morality either, then we end up relying on whatever 'feels right' to this Authority. So *morality still ends up dependent on subjective preference or choice, but now it's the subjective preference or choice of the Authority rather than the individual.* The introduction of an external moral Authority into the picture merely provides the *illusion* of increased objectivity. It's unclear why this is any improvement. Indeed, reliance on Authority may result in a rather more dangerous situation. At least within a more Liberal regime individuals have the opportunity (indeed, they are encouraged) to monitor and correct each other. A powerful moral Authority is unlikely to be corrected by anyone but him or herself.

Secondly, in any case, the range of moral positions left open even after it's conceded that morality cannot be given a wholly rational foundation is far narrower than many suppose. As they're usually manifested, Nazism, sexism, slave ownership and homophobia just aren't options. For these beliefs are historically embedded within moral belief systems that involve all sorts of deep logical inconsistencies and flaws that reason is able to expose (we have already seen some examples). Almost everyone signs up to certain basic, fundamentally similar moral principles (yes, even the Nazis – even Hitler claimed he was doing his Christian duty) that then effectively limit the range of moral belief systems open to them. By focusing on the differences between us, we can easily overlook just how much we have in common. And *what we have in common will often rationally settle which of us is right and which is wrong when it comes to what's morally in dispute.*

Thirdly, even if it's true that, when it comes to morality, we must ultimately rely as much on feeling as on reason, *feelings are educable.* We can learn to be more empathetic, more able to discern the character of our own feelings, better at judging whether or not our feelings are appropriate and how they may be distorting our judgement, and so on. So even if emotion does inevitably make a contribution towards an individual's moral judgement, *it certainly doesn't follow that this contribution must inevitably be shallow and self-serving.* Moreover, as we saw in chapter three (and as the director of Antidote, a British organization that aims to foster the development of emotional literacy through schools, recently pointed out[8]), a philosophical, Liberal approach to moral education *can make an important contribution to developing this kind of emotional sophistication and literacy.*

Conclusion

It may be that reason is ultimately incapable of providing morality with a foundation. But, as we've seen in this chapter, *reason still has a vitally important role to play when it comes to determining what's right and what's wrong.* Which is why it remains vitally important that citizens are trained and encouraged to apply their powers of reason to moral questions.

Ten

How do we become good? One increasingly popular answer emphasizes the importance of *building character* by instilling *good habits*. It runs roughly as follows.

Being good and living well are skills, just like, say, being able to ride a bike or play the piano. And skills are primarily acquired, not through *thinking*, but by *doing*. Just as we cannot intellectually work out how to ride a bike, and then hop aboard and confidently cycle off in style, so neither can we intellectually figure out how to be good and then immediately proceed to behave well. If we want people to behave well, we need to drill into them the right behavioural dispositions. It's in having such dispositions that having 'good character' consists, and it's on instilling those dispositions that 'character education' focuses.

This chapter takes a closer look at character education, which, on the face of it, might seem to be at odds with the Liberal approach advocated here.

William James on Good Habits

In his *The Principles of Psychology*, the philosopher James (1890: 121) emphasizes how important good habits are to living well. He begins with a comical illustration of the force of habit:

> There is a story, which is credible enough, though it may not be true, of a practical joker, who, seeing a discharged veteran

carrying home his dinner, suddenly called out, 'Attention!' whereupon the man instantly brought his hands down, and lost his mutton and potatoes in the gutter. The drill had been thorough, and its effects had become embodied in the man's nervous structure.

James believes that, just as soldiers are drilled to obey commands to the point where doing so becomes automatic and unthinking, so we should similarly drill ourselves in behaving in ways advantageous to us.

> The great thing ... in all education, is to make our nervous system our ally instead of our enemy ... For this we must make automatic and habitual, as early as possible, as many useful actions as we can ... The more of the details of our daily life we can hand over to the effortless custody of automatism, the more our higher powers of mind will be set free for their own proper work (James 1890: 122).

It's particularly important, thinks James, that positive habits are ingrained at a young age. The mechanism by which our nervous systems become disposed to act in our interests is *repetition*. The more we make ourselves do something, thinks James, the more we will become *disposed* to do it.

James believes that it's by this kind of repetitive drilling that good character is properly developed. If we want to behave well, the mere desire or intention to act well is not enough. We must instil the right habits in ourselves, so that good behaviour becomes unthinking and automatic.

> No matter how full a reservoir of *maxims* one may possess, and no matter how good one's *sentiments* may be, if one has not taken advantage of every concrete opportunity to *act*, one's character may remain entirely unaffected for the better. With mere good intentions, hell is proverbially paved (James 1890: 125).

James argues that, unless the right habits are ingrained in us from early on, by constant repetition, so that good behaviour becomes unthinking and automatic, the fabric of society is under threat. Habit is 'the enormous flywheel of society, its most precious conservative agent. It alone is what keeps us all within the bounds of ordinance' (James 1890: 121).

Aristotle

Aristotle, like James, also emphasizes the importance of instilling good habits. Aristotle's thinking is particularly influential in today's 'character education' movement.

Aristotle thought that while we aren't naturally virtuous, we can become so. The right way to raise a child, according to Aristotle, involves inculcating certain habits or customs of behaviour. We must be *trained* to act well by getting into the habit of doing it, so that such behaviour becomes part of our nature. So that it becomes, if you like, *second* nature.

Aristotle does not believe children will spontaneously develop such virtuous character traits as honesty, integrity, generosity, fortitude, perseverance and orderliness. Their nature, to begin with, is to do whatever they feel like doing. They are led by their own immediate fancies and whims. It's only by being trained, by some external authority, to behave well that they will acquire the habit of behaving virtuously.

However, unlike James, Aristotle is not after mindless, automatic behaviour. As Broadie (1991: 109), the author of *Ethics With Aristotle*, explains, Aristotle's view is that

[f]orming a habit is connected with repetition, but where what is repeated are (for example) just acts, habituation cannot be a mindless process, and the habit (once formed) of acting justly cannot be blind in its operations, since one needs intelligence to see why different things are just in different circumstances. So far as habit plays a part, it is not that of autopilot ...

What we should get into the habit of doing is reflecting and applying our intelligence in order to arrive at the right judgement, and then acting upon it. This is obviously not something we can do unthinkingly. Our minds need actively to be engaged.

As Broadie points out, there's a further reason why it would be a mistake to characterize Aristotle as recommending we turn citizens into unthinking automata or mindless creatures of habit. By getting into the habit of behaving well, so that it becomes second nature to us, we are able to learn two valuable lessons.

First, we learn that behaving in these ways is good. This is not something that can simply be figured out in a purely intellectual way. We need personal experience of what living virtuously is like before we are in a position to appreciate that this really is how we ought to behave. And we are only able to have that experience if we have been trained, disciplined and habituated into acting well by some external authority. It's only by doing it, by being forced into the habit of doing it, that we are able to recognize for ourselves that this is how we should live.

Secondly, having been properly trained, we are also released from the grip of our own immediate desires, and so we are now also *able* to live that way. So it seems an individual trained in the way Aristotle recommends acquires both a kind of knowledge and a kind of freedom that the child left to his or her own devices will never attain.

Character Education

There's a great deal of intuitive plausibility to Aristotle's vision of what a good moral education involves. There's undoubtedly some truth to the suggestion that individuals can't be expected simply to *reason* their way to being good, that they must get into the right habits before they are in a position to judge. But then shouldn't moral education, in the first instance, be about not getting them to think and *reason*, but about developing good character by instilling *good habits*?

That moral education needs to be rooted in the instilling of good habits is, as I say, an increasingly popular point of view. Numerous books have been written to help parents and schools build character, including best-sellers like Lickona's (2004) *Character Matters – How to Help Our Children Develop Good Judgement, Integrity, and Other Essential Virtues*, Isaacs' (1984) *Character Building – A Guide for Parents and Teachers*, and LeGette's (1999) *Parents, Kids and Character: 21 Strategies to Help Your Children Develop Good Character*.

In the US, character-building has caught the popular and political imagination. Many see it as the cure for the moral malaise. Lickona (2004: xxiii), for example, says that:

> The premise of the character education movement is that the disturbing behaviours that bombard us daily – violence, greed, corruption, incivility, drug abuse, sexual immorality, and a poor work ethic – have a common core: the absence of good character. Educating for character, unlike piecemeal reforms, goes beneath the symptoms to the root of these problems. It therefore offers the best hope of improvement in all these areas.

Indeed, character education has become a focus of both the Democrat and Republican parties. George Bush's plan for education, *No Child Left Behind*, specifically refers to character education, stating that

> additional funds will be provided for Character Education grants to states and districts to train teachers in methods of incorporating character-building lessons and activities into the classroom.[1]

Character education has, according to one proponent, Ryan (1989), become the 'new moral education'.

> The new moral education is not a fad. Instead, it is a break with the faddism that characterized much of the moral education of the Sixties and the Seventies, when the emphasis was on process and teachers pretended that the culture has few moral principles or lessons to transmit. ... [T]he new moral education is really quite old; indeed, it is deeply rooted in classical thinking about education. [Some of it] comes straight from Aristotle's *Nicomachean Ethics*. Aristotle said that a man becomes virtuous by performing virtuous acts; he becomes kind by doing kind acts; he becomes brave by doing brave acts. A school that institutes a community service programme is merely operationalizing Aristotle. And a teacher who takes on the new moral education is simply reassuming a responsibility traditionally assigned to teachers. The role of the school is not simply to make children smart, but to make them smart *and* good. We must help children

acquire the skills, the attitudes, and the dispositions that will help them live well and that will enable the common good to flourish. For schools and teachers to do only half the job puts the individual child and all the rest of us in danger.

Proponents of character education suggest there's growing evidence that character-building programmes are effective, and that they can even help improve academic results.[2] The building of character is increasingly seen, not as an optional extra that might be added to the curriculum, but as the framework within which good teaching takes place. Schools with character-building programmes are, it seems, more effective schools. There's certainly a great deal of anecdotal evidence that character-building programmes can work. Here, for example, is Hal Urban, a high school teacher, testifying to the power of character education to transform a school:

> I've had the good fortune to visit schools all over the country that have character education programmes in place. The first word that pops into my mind when I visit them is 'clean'. I see clean campuses and buildings, hear clean language, and see kids dressed cleanly and neatly. I see courtesy being practiced by everyone – students, teachers, administrators, custodians, and cafeteria workers. Most important, I see teaching and learning going on in an atmosphere that is caring, positive, and productive (quoted in Lickona 2004: xxvi).

An Attack on the Liberal Approach

But if character education is the way forward, doesn't that mean giving up on the kind of Liberal approach advocated in this book? Surely the Liberal approach, with its emphasis on individual autonomy and the use of reason, has now quite rightly been superseded by character education, which places the emphasis where it should be – on *doing*, rather than on *thinking*. Surely we need to cultivate good habits precisely so that individuals *don't* have to start reflecting on what to do.

Defending the Liberal Approach

The attack sketched out in the preceding paragraph commits the fallacy known as *false dilemma*. It insists we choose between two alternatives that are, in fact, entirely compatible. We can have both character education *and* a Liberal approach.

Certainly, the Liberal approach outlined in chapter three doesn't rule out character education. Its focus is on freedom of thought, not freedom of action. Its consistent with a strict, disciplined upbringing. It's also entirely consistent with drilling and the instilling of good habits. You'll remember that Liberalia High, a school that adopts a highly Liberal attitude to moral education, is just as regimented and disciplined as Authoritia High. We can enforce good habits, applying authority with a small 'a', while at the same time encouraging a critical, questioning attitude. We can say that, while we might expect students to behave in certain ways, we certainly don't wish them to swallow whatever we say blindly and uncritically.

So the Liberal approach to moral education is consistent with character education. Indeed, it *requires* it, for at least two reasons:

(i) The kind of Liberal approach advocated in this book can only work within a fairly disciplined environment where children have gotten into the habit of listening to different points of view, calmly and carefully considering them, and so on. So it seems that the Liberal approach does inevitably need to be paired with something like character education.

(ii) One of the virtues we should be promoting is that of thinking critically and independently and getting individuals to take seriously their responsibility for making moral judgements. But, to be effective, this is something we need, not just to *tell* them about, but to get them into the *habit* of doing, so that it too becomes second nature. In which case an effective Liberal moral education must inevitably involve an element of character education.

So, yes, the Liberal approach needs to be paired with character education. But the reverse is also true: character education needs to be paired with the Liberal approach.

One obvious potential problem with 'character education' is that it can be used to ingrain not just noble and virtuous attitudes, but racist and sexist attitudes too. Suppose we ingrain in our young the habit of treating women as domestic serfs. If our offspring are raised to treat women in this way, without much exposure to critical thinking, no doubt they will find the belief that a woman's place is behind the sink 'obvious' and will in turn pass it onto their children. In this way, such 'obvious' beliefs as that women should stay in the home and that Jews are untrustworthy will merrily cascade down the generations without ever being effectively challenged. The 'character' each generation develops will be sexist and racist.

An important safeguard against this potential problem with character education is to add a further habit to the list of habits character education should aim to instil: *the habit of thinking carefully and critically about our own beliefs and attitudes.*

I stress this needs to be a *habit*, a habit introduced fairly early on. If its introduction is delayed until those sexist and racist beliefs and attitudes have got themselves fully ingrained in the child's character, it will then be very difficult to get them out again. If independent, critical thought is not encouraged until late on in the child's development, and if it is then only tokenistic and not habitual, it's unlikely to be of much benefit. The safeguard won't work.

So, far from being in opposition, character education and the kind of Liberal approach to moral education advocated in this book actually complement one another.

Two Types of 'Character Education'

Many proponents of character education are clear that it's both compatible and desirable that it be paired with the fostering of independent critical thought. But not all. For some, 'character education' is merely a useful banner under which they hope to reinstate religious Authority with a capital 'A'. They want the opportunity to drill children into mindlessly accepting their own religious and moral beliefs. They are looking to instil specifically religious habits, to get them ingrained in children while their intellects are firmly switched off.

Advocates of character education are aware of such divisions within their ranks. Take, for example, this quote from an article at the character education website, www.goodcharacter.com.

> What is character education? This is a highly controversial issue, and depends largely on your desired outcome. Many people believe that simply getting kids to do what they're told is character education. This idea often leads to an imposed set of rules and a system of rewards and punishments that produce temporary and limited behavioural changes, but they do little or nothing to affect the underlying character of the children. There are others who argue that our aim should be to develop independent thinkers who are committed to moral principles in their lives, and who are likely to do the right thing even under challenging circumstances. That requires a somewhat different approach.[3]

It does require a different approach – a Liberal approach.

We should be wary of allowing those wishing to return to more Authority-based forms of values education to hijack character education. Some proponents of character education are, in reality, merely looking for an excuse to turn children into moral sheep with a religious Authority leading the flock.

Those enthusiasts for character education who are, in truth, closet Authoritarians are fond of draping themselves with Aristotle's intellectual mantle. The irony is that Aristotle was no Authoritarian. Yes, Aristotle emphasizes the importance of applying authority with a small 'a', so that the right habits can be instilled. But Aristotle's aim in doing so is to get individuals in a position *rationally to recognize for themselves* from personal experience that this is the right way to live. Aristotle's idea is *not* to get individuals blindly to accept whatever Authority tells them.

So let's say yes to character education, but let's be clear that it needs to be Liberal character education, not Authoritarian.

The War for Children's Minds

Eleven

It's often said that, as religious tradition has withered, so the bonds that once held us together as communities have fallen away. We Westerners have become atomized: free-floating, isolated individuals adrift within a moral vacuum, now focused on little more than satisfying our own immediate desires, with no external compass by which to tell right from wrong. As a result, the social fabric is crumbling and immorality and crime are spiralling out of control. If we are to rebuild, we will need religious tradition as our foundation. But doesn't this, in turn, require that we reject the Liberal approach to moral education and return to traditional religious-Authority-based methods instead?

This chapter explains why the correct answer to this question is 'No'.

The Unavoidability of Tradition

Why has religious tradition collapsed? Many believe the seventeenth and eighteenth century Enlightenment revolt against Authority and tradition was a pivotal period. We have seen, for example, that Kant believed that, through the application of pure, unadulterated reason, an individual could figure out what is right and what is wrong without having to appeal to any external tradition or Authority. But can this be done?

Many think not. We saw in chapter nine that Hume denies that reason is ultimately capable of supporting any moral conclusions. Another, rather different objection to the view that morality can be given a wholly rational, tradition-free foundation is that *reason is itself dependent upon tradition*. The philosopher Alisdair MacIntyre argues that it's not possible for an individual to conjure morality out of thin air, independently of any tradition. Indeed, according to MacIntyre, whatever forms of reasoning we employ are themselves born of and dependent upon tradition. So it's actually impossible to do what Kant attempted to do: to apply reason on an individual basis, independently of any tradition.

> [A]ll reasoning takes place within the context of some traditional mode of thought (MacIntyre 1985: 222).

There is no possibility of my 'stepping outside' of all tradition and thinking from a tradition-free perspective, for what I am

> is in key part what I inherit, a specific past that is present to some degree in my present. I find myself part of a history and that is generally to say, whether I like it or not, whether I recognize it or not, one of the bearers of a tradition (MacIntyre 1985: 221).

The new Pontiff, Pope Benedict, echoes MacIntyre when he attacks the suggestion that we rely on 'autonomous reason' in making moral judgements. While not against the use of reason, the Pope believes reason must necessarily be paired with a faith tradition.

> When a strict autonomous reason, which does not want to know anything about the faith, tries to get out of the bog of uncertainty 'by pulling itself up by its hair', to express it in some way, it will be difficult for this effort to succeed. For human reason is not autonomous in absolute [*sic*]. It is always found in a historical context (Ratzinger 2005).

Some will conclude that if MacIntyre and the Pope are right, then the kind of Liberal approach to moral education outlined in chapter three – an approach that emphasizes the importance of individual autonomy and reason – must be untenable.

Losing the Plot

MacIntyre also emphasizes the way in which morality is rooted in *stories*:

> I can only answer the question 'What am I to do?' if I can answer the prior question, 'Of what story or stories do I find myself a part?' We enter human society, that is, with one or more imputed characters – roles which we have been drafted – and we have to learn what they are in order to be able to understand how others respond to us and how our responses are to be construed. It is through hearing stories ... that children learn or mislearn both what a child and what a parent is, what the cast of characters may be in the drama into which they have been born and what the ways of the world are. Deprive children of stories and you leave them unscripted, anxious stutterers in their actions as in their words (MacIntyre 1985: 216).

In his Richard Dimbleby Lecture (2002), The Archbishop of Canterbury, Rowan Williams, echoes MacIntyre's comments on the importance of a shared narrative. Williams says,

> People learn how to tell the story of their own lives in a coherent way when they have some broader picture to which to relate it. You can only tell the story of your own life, it seems, when it isn't just your story, or even the story of those immediately close to you.

Many would concur: without a traditional, shared story to sustain them, morality and meaning wither away. As we have lost touch with the great religious story in which Western morality is rooted, so we are also losing our grip on the values embedded in it. We are, quite literally, losing the plot.

Rowan Williams on the Importance of Religious Tradition

Rowan Williams also makes a further, related point. He says, 'Let me put it provocatively. We are no longer confident of educating children in a tradition.' And yet, continues the Archbishop, a religious tradition is necessary if we want to avoid ending up thinking of everything only in terms of our own individual desires. Without a religious tradition, says Williams, society degenerates into little more than a 'marketplace' governing our competing short-term individual interests and preferences. All larger questions are forgotten. In fact, Williams argues that it's only from the perspective of a religious tradition that questions about the *meaning* of our lives even get raised, let alone answered. While we don't want tradition entirely to dominate the present, what, asks Williams (2002), about the person who

> is now able to inhabit a tradition with confidence, fully aware
> that it isn't the only possible perspective on persons and things,
> but equally aware that they are part of a network of relations
> and conventions far wider than what is instantly visible or even
> instantly profitable, and this network is inseparable from who they
> concretely are? I suspect that many of us would recognize in this
> more of freedom than of slavery, because it makes possible a real
> questioning of the immediate agenda of a society, the choices that
> are defined and managed for you by the market.

Must We Abandon the Liberal Approach?

But doesn't all this spell disaster for the Liberal approach outlined in chapter three? Doesn't that approach to moral education encourage individuals to reject all traditions and associated narratives and apply reason in a wholly tradition-free way? And if this is undesirable, as the Archbishop of Canterbury suggests, or even impossible, as MacIntyre and the Pope contend, must we not then reject that Liberal approach?

No. Let's go through these objections one by one, beginning with Rowan Williams' insistence that without a religious tradition, the bigger questions simply won't even get asked, let alone answered.

Response to Williams

As a secular philosopher who has spent half a lifetime asking such questions as whether there's a God, whether life has meaning, what makes things right and wrong, whether there may be life after death, and whether there is anything beyond the material, I find it surprising that the Archbishop of Canterbury insists that it's only from the perspective of a religious tradition that such questions ever get asked. The great religious traditions do not have a monopoly on addressing the most fundamental and challenging issues. They share that honour with the secular, *philosophical* tradition. And one advantage of a more philosophical approach to such questions (which certainly doesn't *rule out* religious answers, of course) is that it doesn't prejudge the issue. Rather than approaching such questions in a genuinely critical, open-minded way, religious enquirers have sometimes already made up their minds: they've already decided that only a religious answer will do. In the hands of the faithful, questions like 'What is the meaning of life?' may be asked, not in the spirit of sincere, open-minded enquiry, but merely as the opening gambit in an attempt to recruit more true believers.

But even if Williams were right – even if it were true that it's only from a religious perspective that such big questions ever get asked – that would only give us a reason to raise children within a religious tradition. It would not give us a justification for insisting on an Authority-based religious education. Quite the opposite. For *the Authoritarian approach actually involves shutting down the kind of debate Williams wants to stimulate.*

So it seems Williams has actually given us a powerful argument for *favouring* a Liberal approach to religious and moral education – an approach that actively encourages independent critical thought about these big questions (which, I should add, Williams may himself be happy to admit).

'Nothing Can Claim Exemption From Reflective Critique'

What of MacIntyre's point that Kant is wrong to suppose reason can be applied independently of all tradition (because every application of reason is inevitably rooted in some tradition or other)? Doesn't that, in effect, spell doom for the Liberal approach recommended here? For isn't the Liberal approach all about individuals applying reason for themselves, *independently of any tradition*?

No, it isn't. We're not defending the view that reason alone can conjure up morality all by itself (as I explained in chapter one). What we're defending is the view that children, and indeed adults, should be encouraged and trained to think critically about the tradition in which they find themselves. Pointing out that reason cannot be applied independently of all tradition does nothing to undermine this point. MacIntyre himself agrees that '[n]othing can claim exemption from reflective critique' (Horton and Mendus 1994: 289). In applying reason, we may look to and draw upon a tradition. MacIntyre may even be right that we *have* to. But that's not to say we should be encouraged, at any stage, blindly and unquestioningly to accept our tradition's moral principles, not even when we are young. We have not yet been given any reason to suppose that autonomous critical thinking is something that should, at *any* stage, be discouraged.[1]

The Importance of Stories

What of MacIntyre's point, echoed by Williams, that morality is intertwined with and rooted in stories? Doesn't this tend to undermine the Liberal approach advocated here, which places the emphasis on reason?

Again, no. No doubt children should know about and understand their own cultural heritage. To make sense of their own culture, children do need to be familiar with their own tradition and those stories that partly constitute it. So of course they should be taught that tradition and those stories. A Liberal need have no difficulty with that. But to acknowledge the importance of stories and tradition is not to downplay the role of reason and a critical approach. The two are compatible. Many of those teachers now using philosophy in the classroom also emphasize the importance of stories. They agree that telling and thinking about stories has an important role to play in a child's moral development. Stories provide a focus for thought and discussion. There's no reason why these stories couldn't be, say, Bible stories.

So a Liberal need have no objection to the use of stories, even specifically *religious* stories, in the teaching of morality. What the Liberal rejects is simply the suggestion that we should aim to instil a largely uncritical, deferential attitude in those to whom these stories and traditions are taught. We have not, in this chapter, been given any reason to suppose the Liberal is wrong about that. Nor have we been given any reason to move in the direction of Authority-based moral education. If anything, the case for the kind of Liberal moral education of the sort outlined in chapter three has been strengthened (by Rowan Williams).

Community, Religion and Authority

So far, this chapter has dispensed with a few common worries about the Liberal approach to moral education. Let's now move on to a rather different, and perhaps more substantial, line of argument. Many believe it was our shared faith traditions that once bound us together into moral, mutually supportive communities. They claim it is only by revitalizing these traditions that we can regain that sense of community and belonging.

There is a grain of truth to this. It does seem that religious communities really are more stable and longer lasting than are secular communities, as the British philosopher Blackburn (2004: 18) (an atheist) admits:

> One of the more depressing findings of social anthropology is that
> societies professing a religion are more stable, and last longer,
> than those that do not. It is estimated that breakaway groups like
> communes or new age communities last some four times longer
> if they profess a common religion than if they do not.

There is, it appears, good empirical evidence that religious belief helps build and sustain communities (see, for example, Stark and Bainbridge 1997).

But, as we've seen, the Liberal approach is not anti-religious. It's compatible with a religious education that positively argues for a specific set of religious values. A religious moral education and upbringing does not have to be Authority-based. So, even if it's admitted that religion is important for sound, stable communities, that by itself would not provide us with a reason to favour a more Authority-based approach to moral and religious education.

But perhaps this would be to reject the community-building argument too quickly. For what, if what increases the stability of a society and binds its members more tightly together is not so much religion *per se* as specifically *Authoritarian* religion. What if it's the Authority residing in a religion that really does the binding? In that case, getting individuals to apply their own powers of reason will tend to have a corrosive effect. It will tend to loosen those social bonds that religious Authority has forged.

Blackburn acknowledges this. He says that the reason why sprinkling religious 'fairy dust' on a set of beliefs has the effect of binding a band of believers together more tightly is that it acts to 'close off questions and doubts, and in effect fend off reason', making it all the more difficult for any individual to break step with their community. It's the Authoritarian character of religion that makes it such a highly effective social adhesive.

Perhaps that shouldn't surprise us. No doubt a community of religious believers whose minds are collectively bound by a powerful Authority will always tend to be rather more tightly knit than its Liberal equivalent, and even its *religious* Liberal equivalent. So let's admit that religious Authority is, if you like, the super glue of social engineering. The question is: does the sheer power of religious Authority to fuse people together into communities justify us in applying it?

Surely not. To say that religious Authority is a powerful social adhesive is not to say that it's the *only* social adhesive, or that we can't build stable communities without it. While there are steps we might take to 'rebuild community', it is, to say the least, unclear why we need to reach for the gluepot of religious Authority.

Especially as we know there are alternatives. We have seen, for example, that the kind of Liberal, philosophical approach to teaching morality advocated in chapter three, on which problems, questions and views are freely shared and collectively examined and discussed, can also help foster a sense of community, belonging, respect for and engagement with others. We have even seen that there's a growing body of empirical evidence that it is, in this respect, pretty effective.

Of course, critics will insist that Liberal alternatives to the glue of religious Authority just aren't strong enough to maintain the social fabric. The question is, where's the *evidence* to support this claim? Pointing to the moral malaise and saying 'But look at what happens when religious Authority collapses: so does society' is like arguing for the use of blue asbestos in buildings on the grounds that, when the blue asbestos components of these buildings were removed, the buildings fell down. Just as there are alternatives to the use of toxic asbestos in constructing sound buildings, so there are alternatives to the use of religious Authority in constructing sound communities (even if they won't be *quite* as strong communities built without it).

Personally, I don't want to live in a community glued together by religious Authority, living alongside people whose minds are bound as effectively as their behaviour. I would find that uncomfortably oppressive. We can all agree that community is a good thing, but many of us would consider that too high a price to pay. However, my objection to the use of religious Authority in building communities is not fundamentally one of taste. There are also powerful arguments against the use of religious Authority to build communities, not least of which is that not only are Authority-based communities uncomfortably oppressive, they're dangerous: they tend to produce moral sheep.

But perhaps the most damning objection to the use of religious Authority for social-engineering purposes is that at the same time as a religious Authority binds the members of a community more tightly together, it creates far wider chasms *between* communities. As Ignatieff (1993: 188) reminds us,

[t]he more strongly you feel the bonds of belonging to your own group, the more hostile, the more violent will your feelings be towards outsiders.

This divisive result is likely to be even more calamitous when the group in question is governed by a religious Authority. The increase in the magnetic attraction between the members of a community generated by their allegiance to a shared religious Authority will inevitably be accompanied by a corresponding repulsion towards those outside, whose failure to defer to the insiders' own divinely sanctioned Authority will, from the perspective of an insider, make those outsiders seem increasingly corrupt and beyond the pale.

And so, ironically, in a country with more than one religion, the effect of reaching for the glue pot of Authoritarian religion is likely to be a society that is more deeply fractured, not less. Indeed, *the more Authoritarian that religion is, the deeper those fractures are likely to be.*

Gray on de Maistre: 'Reason Dissolves Civilization'

Some suggest that getting individuals to reason even about their most fundamental moral and religious beliefs is dangerously corrosive: it will inevitably end up eroding those values upon which civilization rests. Gray (1995b), in his book *Isaiah Berlin*, says about Count Joseph de Maistre (1753–1821), a staunch defender of the Authority of the Church and the Pope and one of the Enlightenment's most trenchant critics, that,

> [w]hen he represents reason and analysis as corrosive and destructive, solvents of custom and allegiance that cannot replace the bonds of sentiment and tradition which they weaken and demolish, he illuminates, better perhaps than any subsequent writer, the absurdity of the Enlightenment faith (for such it undoubtedly was) that human society can have a rational foundation. If to reason is to question, then questioning will have no end, until it has wrought the dissolution of the civilization that gave it birth (Gray 1995b: 125–126).

This remains a popular criticism of both the Enlightenment and the kind of Liberal approach to moral education advocated here. We should dissuade people from thinking and questioning too deeply and independently about fundamentals, for they'll end up undermining the values upon which our society depends.

Is the criticism fair? Again, let's concede, if only for the sake of argument, that morality can't be given a wholly rational foundation. Certainly, it's naive to suppose, as Kant and some other (though not all) Enlightenment thinkers did, that reason is capable of answering all our moral questions. No doubt de Maistre and Gray are right to say that society cannot have a wholly rational foundation either, given the way morality and society are intertwined.

But of course, as we've seen, this concession leaves untouched the key Liberal principle – the principle Kant himself takes to be definitive of Enlightenment – that, when it comes to morality, individuals should be encouraged to think critically and for themselves, rather than defer more-or-less unquestioningly to tradition and Authority. We can sign up to this principle without buying into the Enlightenment doctrine Gray dismisses as 'absurd'.

Why does de Maistre suppose that the relentless application of reason must inevitably be corrosive and destructive?

Actually, it's obviously false that the effect of applying reason to moral belief is inevitably destructive. De Maistre, in effect, acknowledges this by attempting to construct a rational argument in support of his claim that we ought to defer to Authority – itself a moral claim. Ironically, de Maistre's own argument requires that reason does indeed possess at least some power to reveal moral truths.

There's no denying reason can be destructive, of course. It's certainly capable of undermining moral positions. But reason undermines only those moral positions that deserve to be undermined, because, for example, they are fundamentally inconsistent, involve spurious reasoning (for example, if they morally condemn homosexuality on the grounds that it's 'unnatural') or are based on false claims (about the intelligence of women or the character of Jews, for example).

True, as we saw in chapter ten, it seems we may inevitably arrive at a point where reason inevitably runs out of steam when it comes to justifying a moral position. An individual who applies their own powers of reason to the prevailing morality will quickly dig down to its moral foundations. They may then find that these foundations are not, and cannot be, rationally underpinned. But of course, if reason is ultimately incapable of underpinning our most basic moral beliefs by showing them to be true, *neither is it capable of undermining them by showing them to be false.*

De Maistre and Gray also forget that to question is not to reject. The average moral philosopher spends years questioning his or her own moral beliefs and traditions, subjecting them to the minutest critical scrutiny. Yet that philosopher will invariably end up retaining much, if not all, of what they started with. The same is true of many religious believers. They may have thought long and hard about their religious belief, and questioned their most fundamental convictions. Yet those convictions have emerged unscathed. Indeed, a belief that has survived the test of reason may grow stronger and its adherents may become all the more committed in its defence.

Defenders of Authority, like de Maistre, have always been quick to warn that if individuals are allowed to think too freely, they will inevitably unravel the very fabric of civilization. What's still missing is a decent argument in support of this apocalyptic claim.

Indeed, it's rather ironic that de Maistre insists that unless reason is shackled, and the Authority of the Church and the Pope upheld, the bonds that hold society together will unravel. Much the same justification was used to defend the persecution of the early Christian Church. At one time, Christianity was itself a revolutionary system of belief. As Mill (1991) points out, the justification offered by Emperor Marcus Aurelius for persecuting the early Christians was precisely that their revolutionary belief system threatened to dissolve those ties that knit society together.

As a ruler of mankind, [Marcus Aurelius] deemed it his duty not to suffer society to fall in pieces; and saw not how, if its existing ties were removed, any others could be formed which could again knit it together. The new religion openly aimed at dissolving these ties: unless, therefore, it was his duty to adopt that religion, it was his duty to put it down (Mill 1991: 31).

The old chestnut that new-fangled ideas will end up unravelling the social fabric, with disastrous consequences, has been the knee-jerk reaction of social conservatives since the dawn of time. What they more often as not fail to supply is much evidence that it's true.

Sacks on Tradition

Of course, not every defender of Authority-based moral education wants to turn us into unthinking automata blindly treading whatever path tradition lays down. This is certainly true of Sacks and Phillips, for example. It would be unfair to caricature them as wanting to transform us into lobotomized slaves of tradition.

Still, while hardly anyone is recommending complete, blind, unswerving loyalty to whatever tradition dictates, it is clear that Sacks, Phillips and many others believe the young should, in the first instance, adopt an attitude of deference to what they both call 'external authority' on moral questions. Independent critical thought is only to be allowed when individuals have been fully and properly immersed within the tradition.

Sacks, for example, says that before we can properly criticize a practice, we need to set foot within it, 'finding our way round it from the inside'. This, says Sacks (1997: 176–177),

> presupposes distinctive attitudes: authority, obedience, discipline, persistence and self-control. ... There is a stage at which we put these rules to the test. We assert our independence, we challenge, ask for explanations, occasionally rebel and try other ways of doing things. Eventually we reach an equilibrium ... For the most part ... we stay within the world as we have inherited it. ... capable now of self-critical reflection on its strengths and weaknesses, perhaps working to change it from within, but recognizing that its rules are not a constraint but the very possibility of shared

> experiences and relationship and communication ... autonomy
> takes place *within* a tradition.

So Sacks acknowledges the importance, in a mature citizen, of a critical, reflective stance towards his or her own tradition. But he emphasizes that we must first be fully immersed in that tradition. And he stresses the importance of deference to Authority in the earlier stages of assimilation. He believes that

> autonomy – the capacity to act and choose in the consciousness of
> alternatives – is a late stage in moral development ... It is not
> where it begins (Sacks 1997: 177).

What Sacks means by 'a late stage' is unclear. At what point is Sacks willing to let individuals adopt a more reflective, critical stance towards their own tradition? At 11? At 15? At 25? It's hard to say. In fact it's not at all obvious whether reflective, critical examination of the tradition in which you are brought up is something Sacks would at any stage be willing to *encourage*. It's merely something he thinks will spontaneously happen at some 'late stage'.

So, while Sacks is prepared to tolerate some freedom of thought and expression at some unspecified point in the individual's development, it's clear Sacks wants moral education to be much more Authority-based than it currently is (or at least as it is outside the more conservative religious schools). He believes more emphasis should be placed on more-or-less uncritical deference to Authority than it should on independent critical thought (at least until some 'late stage'). So, as we have defined Authoritarian with a capital 'A', Sacks is an Authoritarian (though it's possible to be far more Authoritarian than Sacks – Sacks may be on the Authoritarian side of the Liberal/Authoritarian scale, but he's not at that extreme end of the scale). Sacks would oppose the highly Liberal approach to moral and religious education advocated in chapter three. He wants schools more like Authoritia High, less like Liberalia High.

The question is: why is more-or-less blind, uncritical acceptance of the pronouncements of Authority required at any stage?

Why does raising individuals 'within a tradition' require that we begin by stifling their freedom to think and question?

Sacks cites MacIntyre in support of his Authoritarian stance on moral and religious education. But MacIntyre's plausible point that reason is inevitably rooted in tradition – that it cannot be applied independently of any tradition – does not require that individuals should be discouraged from applying their own powers of reason *once they are able*. And it is clear from the kind of studies looked at in chapter three that children are remarkably adept at applying their critical faculties to moral questions from very early on. Some immersion in a tradition may indeed be required before their critical faculties can be properly engaged. But once they are engaged, once children are striving to engage them, once they are beginning actively to question and explore (which does come very naturally to them), what then is the case for preventing children from applying their critical faculties to moral and religious beliefs? Particularly until, as Sacks puts it, some 'late stage'? For if we are to restrict the child's ability to think and question until some 'late stage', we're going to have to actively suppress this natural tendency. In fact it's hard to see how we're to avoid relying pretty heavily on the kinds of psychological manipulation outlined back in chapter three.

So, though this is no doubt not quite what he intended, what Sacks extracts from MacIntyre's point about tradition amounts, in effect, to an open-ended invitation to shut down the critical faculties of young people long enough to get them heavily religiously indoctrinated. Sacks leaves the door open for Authoritarians to engage in *years and years* of religious programming, sending new citizens out into the moral world intellectually armed with little more than a tokenistic, last-minute bit of critical reflection grudgingly tolerated at some 'late stage'.

As I say, I'm sure such an invitation is not quite what Sacks is after. Still, whatever Authoritarian form of moral and religious education Sacks would himself recommend, it seems clear that MacIntyre's plausible point about the impossibility of applying reason independently of any tradition fails to support it.

Authoritarians and Communitarians

Those who call themselves, or are called by others, 'communitarians', stress the importance of community and tradition to maintaining the social fabric. Among these 'communitarians' you will often find a number of religious Authoritarians who believe that the kind of broadly communitarian points and arguments outlined in this chapter support their call for a more Authority-based approach to moral and religious education. The truth, however, is that while there may be some truth to communitarianism, none of the arguments examined here justifies any such lurch in the direction of Authority.

Indeed, communitarians can quite consistently be Liberals-with-a-capital-'L'.

Twelve

Many will dismiss the argument developed in this book on the grounds that it ignores human nature. Here's a fictional illustration of the sort of objection I have in mind.

> It's all very well encouraging people to think for themselves about right and wrong. But the cost of this free thinking is unacceptably high. Your advice flies in the face of reality. People, by nature, are driven by 'I want', not 'I ought'. The vast majority are certainly not smart or sophisticated enough to be trusted to reason their way to doing the right thing. Even the most intelligent are likely to use their brainpower to construct some ingenious justification for doing whatever it is that they *want* to do.
>
> The only effective way of getting people to be good is to get them to defer to a religious Authority. And I stress that it needs to be religious Authority. People are only likely to accept the legitimacy of an Authority if they think it has some sort of divine backing. A moral society requires that the masses continue to believe both in God and in some external God-representing Authority to which they feel a powerful obligation to defer.

Of course, the argument set out above doesn't require that God actually exist. It's an argument for the usefulness of belief in God, not its truth. Whether or not the belief is true is quite beside the point.

'He's Making a List, He's Checking it Twice ...'

After all, there are all sorts of belief that, while false, can still be useful. Children are often encouraged to believe in Santa Claus and his 'naughty list' – the roll of misbehaved tykes who won't be getting presents on Christmas Day. They learn that (Coots and Gillespie 1934)

> He's making a list,
> He's checking it twice,
> He's going to find out who's naughty and nice
> Santa Claus is coming to town.

One reason why parents find belief in Santa useful is that he can help keep their children in line. The thought that Santa always keeps a close eye on little Johnny ('He knows when you've been bad or good, so be good for goodness sake') and may even put his name on the naughty list may help maintain Johnny on the straight and narrow. But of course, the fact that Johnny's belief in Santa helps improve Johnny's behaviour doesn't give us, or Johnny, the slightest reason to suppose this belief is actually true.

Notice that in order for the 'naughty list' strategy to be really effective, parents must appear to believe in Santa themselves. The same goes for those who offer the above argument for religious belief. They may agree, in private, that religious belief, like belief in Santa, is false. But they're unlikely to admit it in public. Just as the parent who wants to use belief in Santa to control their child's behaviour will pretend they believe themselves, so the atheist who thinks religion is required to maintain the social fabric is likely to feign religious commitment.

Those who treat religious belief as a tool with which to manipulate others, but not something they are required to embrace themselves, may view themselves as an 'elite': the possessors of a secret that must be kept from the common herd if the manipulation is to succeed. Are there such people? Certainly. Let's take a look at two examples: Machiavelli and Strauss.

Machiavelli

Machiavelli taught that if a ruler – a prince – wishes to maintain the state, he should be prepared to lie, torture, steal, kill and do whatever else is necessary. But he should nevertheless *pretend* always to be merciful, faithful, humane, upright and, above all, religious. Appearing to be pious and religious is of particular importance, according to Machiavelli.

> [A] prince, especially a new one, cannot observe all those things for which men are esteemed, being often forced, in order to maintain the state, to act contrary to faith, friendship, humanity, and religion. ... [But] a prince ought to take care that he never lets anything slip from his lips that is not replete with the above-named five qualities, that he may appear to him who sees and hears him altogether merciful, faithful, humane, upright, and religious. There is nothing more necessary to appear to have than this last quality, inasmuch as men judge generally more by the eye than by the hand. ... Every one sees what you appear to be, few really know what you are ... (Machiavelli 1505).

Machiavelli's advice to rulers about religion is: preach one thing, do another.

Leo Strauss's 'Noble Lies and Pious Frauds'

A more recent figure who also stresses the importance of feigning religious piety is the German political philosopher Leo Strauss. Strauss, a Jewish intellectual who escaped the Nazis in 1938 and ended up teaching at the University of Chicago for over two decades, considered religion a pious fraud but a desirable fraud none-the-less. According to Strauss, the Enlightenment thinkers were mistaken in supposing religious authority and tradition could safely be dispensed with. Religion is important for moral order and stability – without it, relativism and moral chaos are likely to prevail. For this reason, Strauss thought that while the ruling elite need not be religious, they should *pretend* to be religious.

They should also strongly encourage religious belief among the masses.

Many of Strauss's students and his students' students have become highly influential. They are said to include Allen Bloom (1988), Paul Wolfowitz (former Defence Secretary, now President of The World Bank), Supreme Court Nominee Robert Bork, Justice Clarence Thomas, former Secretary of State for Education William Bennett, and former Assistant Secretary of State Alan Keyes.[1] Of course, being a student of Strauss does not make you a Straussian (perhaps none of these individuals would call themselves Straussians). Still, Strauss is widely thought to have many prominent followers within Republican circles. In 1996, *Time* magazine rated Strauss one of the most influential figures in Washington.

Many consider Strauss's influence sinister. Here, for example, is Drury (2004) professor of philosophy and political science at the University of Regina:

> There is a certain irony in the fact that the chief guru of the neoconservatives is a thinker who regarded religion merely as a political tool intended for the masses but not for the superior few. Leo Strauss ... did not dissent from Marx's view that religion is the opium of the people; but he believed that the people need their opium. He therefore taught that those in power must invent noble lies and pious frauds to keep the people in the stupor for which they are supremely fit.

According to Drury, Strauss's neoconservative followers 'dogmatically accept the view of religion as a panacea for everything that ails America'. And this, Drury argues, is profoundly dangerous, not least because

> the use of religion as a political tool encourages the cultivation of an elite of liars and frauds who exempt themselves from the rules they apply to the rest of humanity. And this is a recipe for tyranny, not freedom or democracy.

Whether or not Drury's concern about the potentially dangerous legacy of Strauss's thinking is reasonable, it's certainly interesting to consider to what extent neoconservatives within the current US administration would be willing to agree with Strauss's views on religion. Would some concur with Strauss that, whether or not religion is true, it is nevertheless necessary for the maintenance of a healthy society?

Irving Kristol

Irving Kristol is a contemporary political thinker influenced by Strauss who has also helped to shape the US neoconservative movement (indeed, Kristol is often called the 'godfather of neoconservatism'). Like many conservatives, Kristol believes America is experiencing a culture war between the defenders of traditional religiously-based morality on the one hand and 'liberals' on the other. It was neoconservatives like Kristol that brought the thinking of Strauss into this war.

Kristol (1999: 8) says about Strauss that

> [w]hat made him so controversial within the academic community was his disbelief in the Enlightenment dogma that 'the truth will make men free'. ... Strauss was an intellectual aristocrat who thought that the truth could make *some* minds free, but he was convinced that there was an inherent conflict between philosophic truth and political order, and that the popularization and vulgarization of these truths might import unease, turmoil and the release of popular passions hitherto held in check by tradition and religion with utterly unpredictable, but mostly negative, consequences.

Kristol is quoted as agreeing with Strauss about the dangers of unrestricted access to the truth. 'There are different kinds of truths for different kinds of people,' he is reported as saying.

> There are truths appropriate for children; truths that are appropriate for students; truths that are appropriate for educated adults; and truths that are appropriate for highly educated adults, and the notion that there should be one set of truths available to everyone is a modern democratic fallacy. It doesn't work.[2]

Presumably a similar risk attaches to the unfettered use of reason. Reason is likely to expose the truth, and the truth may turn out to be something only a select few can handle. Indeed, Kristol says that if Strauss is right and God and salvation are indispensable illusions (by the way, unlike Strauss, Kristol never claims they are illusions), then one solution, if we wished, would be to

> let a handful of sages, who know the truth and can live with it, keep it among themselves. Men are then divided into the wise and foolish, the philosophers and the common men, and atheism becomes a guarded esoteric doctrine – for if the illusions of religion were to be discredited, there is no telling with what madness men would be seized, with what uncontrollable anguish. It would indeed become the duty of the wise publicly to defend and support religion, even to call the police power to its aid, while reserving the truth for themselves and their chosen disciples (Kristol 1999: 404).

Not only does Kristol believe that the US needs religion, he thinks it's 'becoming clear' that religious belief is best not considered a private affair.

> I think it is becoming clear that religion ... is far more important politically than the philosophy of liberal individualism admits ... I would go further and say that it is becoming clearer every day that even those who thought they were content with a religion that was a private affair are themselves discovering that such a religion is existentially unsatisfactory (Kristol 1999: 101).

Whether or not religion is false, it's important to keep the masses content and well-behaved. So important, in fact, that Kristol suggests that a liberal, secular society is untenable. Religion must also be woven into the public domain if society is to survive.

The current Bush government has been repeatedly criticized for bringing religion within the sphere of the State – by, for example, changing the rules so that federal funds can be diverted to religious organizations to deliver welfare programmes. Whether or not that's a result of Kristol's influence, I imagine he would approve.

The Dependence of Morality on Religion

But is religious belief indispensable to a healthy and prosperous society? That morality cannot survive without religion is a perennial worry. Even the Enlightenment thinker Voltaire (1694–1778) would not allow his friends to discuss atheism in front of his servants, saying,

> I want my lawyer, tailor, valets, even my wife to believe in God.
> I think that if they do I shall be robbed less and cheated less
> (quoted in Phillips 1996: 191).

Here, too, is Democrat senator Joseph Lieberman echoing George Washington:

> As a people we need to reaffirm our faith and renew the
> dedication of our nation and ourselves to God and God's
> purpose ... George Washington warned us never to 'indulge
> the supposition that morality can be maintained without
> religion'.[3]

We have already seen that even Adolf Hitler insisted that '[s]ecular schools can never be tolerated' because a morality that is not founded on religion is built 'on thin air' (Helmreich 1979: 241).

But of course the claim that morality is causally dependent on religious belief – that it will not (or at least is unlikely to) survive without it – is an empirical hypothesis. It's not enough just to make this claim. We are owed some grounds for believing that it is true. What's the *evidence*?

It's at this point, of course, that reference is typically made to the moral malaise: 'Look,' say the defenders of the view that religion is socially necessary, 'at how religious belief has dwindled since the Enlightenment, and particularly since the Sixties. And look at how, over the same period, amorality and crime have dramatically increased, to the point where the fabric of society is beginning to unravel. Isn't it clear that there is a causal relationship between the two? Isn't it becoming more and more obvious that morality can't be sustained without religion?'

The 'Obviousness' of the Need for Religion

It's not obvious at all. Let's begin by again reminding ourselves that, while there has been a rise in, say, crime and teenage pregnancy, particularly since the 1950s, there have also been some huge moral improvements, including the development of women's rights, the combating of racism, and a growing respect and concern for the environment and the other species with which we share this planet. It's easy to focus on the bad and overlook the good. Conservatives tend to misrepresent any change in morality as a loss of morality. But, having said that, it's undeniable that, say, crime has increased. Can't this be put down to the loss of religious belief?

Establishing a strong causal connection between the loss of religious belief and the rise in crime is not easy. Yes, religious belief may have reduced across the West. But there have been many other changes too. Here's just one example. People are far more mobile, are far less tied to and rooted in a particular local community, than they used to be. Many homes now stand empty during the day. As a result, there's far less awareness of who is up to what down my street. My father tells me that when he was a kid, if he misbehaved a few streets away from his home, the news would be transmitted across the rear garden fences to his mother's back door before he returned through the front. Tightly knit local communities are effective at suppressing delinquency and crime. Their loss is clearly as much due to economic factors as it is any decline in religious belief and practice. And yet it's confidently asserted by neoconservatives that it's the loss of religious belief and practice that is *primarily* to blame for the rise in crime and delinquency. How do they know that?

We've also seen (chapter six) that in the US religious belief hasn't dwindled that much. Ninety-six per cent of Americans still claim to believe in God; forty-three per cent of them say they attend church weekly. In many cases the brand of religion they sign up to is fundamentalist.

And yet, compared to far less religious places like Japan, Canada and Western Europe, the US is in many respects suffering far worse problems in terms of crime and delinquency. It's certainly not *that* obvious that America's problem is fundamentally one of a lack of religion. Nor is it *that* obvious that what it needs above all is even more religion. Perhaps what it needs is more of what Western Europe has got: a decent welfare system and less endemic inequality.

I don't claim that *is* the solution, by the way. I'm merely pointing out that the obviousness of the suggestion that the cure for the West's moral malaise is more religion is debatable, to say the least.

What's also potentially embarrassing for the view that morality can't be sustained without religion is the fact that a great many atheists seem at least as well-behaved and morally concerned as is the typical religious believer. I know it's anecdotal evidence, but I am an atheist, most of my friends are atheists, and none of us seem remotely disposed to dodge our taxes, vandalize phone boxes or steal from the local supermarket. And our kids seem fairly well-adjusted too. In fact, many atheist philosophers (Peter Singer is a fine example) are very passionate ethicists, often *at least* as passionate in their ethical commitments as their religious counterparts.

Doesn't all this rather nail-down the coffin lid on the suggestion that morality can't be sustained without religion?

Arguably not. Neoconservatives typically make one of two moves at this point. The first I call the 'moral capital' move; the second the 'lower orders' move.

The 'Moral Capital' Move

Daniel P. Moloney, the editor of *First Things*, admits in an article in *American Prospect* that atheists are often well-behaved. But he insists this is only because they are living off the accumulated moral capital of traditional religion. When the moral capital of the old religious culture is finally exhausted, morality itself will collapse.

> Religious people are the first to admit that many religious
> people sin often and boldly, and that atheists often act justly.
> They explain these ethical atheists by noting that when atheists
> reject the religion in which they have been raised, they tend to
> keep the morality while discarding its theological foundation.
> Their ethical behaviour is then derivative and parasitic, borrowing

its conscience from a culture permeated by religion; it cannot survive if the surrounding religious culture is not sustained. In short, morality as we know it cannot be maintained without Judeo-Christian religion.[4]

Kristol (1999: 101) agrees:

For well over 150 years now, social critics have been warning us that bourgeoise society was living off the accumulated moral capital of traditional religion and traditional moral philosophy.

Gertrude Himmelfarb (1999: 146) also favours the view that we are

... living off the religious capital of a previous generation and that that capital is being perilously depleted.

So too does Ronald Reagan's Supreme Court nominee Judge Robert K. Bork (1996: 275):

We all know persons without religious belief who nevertheless display all the virtues we associate with religious teaching ... such people are living on the moral capital of prior religious generations ... that moral capital will be used up eventually, having nothing to replenish it, and we will see a culture such as the one we are entering.

This is certainly a convenient explanation for the legions of well-behaved, ethically-committed atheists you'll find living contentedly in places like Canada and Western Europe. The only reason they aren't all amoral degenerates *yet*, and that their societies haven't finally slid into moral oblivion *yet*, is that they're living off the inherited religious capital built up by previous generations. The move is convenient because it renders the claim that morality is dependent upon religion unfalsifiable, at least in the short- to medium-term. No matter how civilized and well-behaved these swathes of ethical atheists might happen to be, they can be sweepingly dismissed with 'Ah, but that's only because the religious capital hasn't run out *yet*'.

But perhaps the most serious difficulty with this move is that it's simply unjustified. Why suppose all these ethically committed atheists are living off the religious capital built up by previous generations, and that this capital must inevitably run out, with disastrous consequences? What's the *evidence* for this claim? We are offered none. Except of course for some vague hand-waving in the direction of the moral malaise. But as it's precisely the moral malaise argument that morality can't be sustained without religion that this 'religious capital' claim is supposed to salvage, the moral malaise argument can't then be used to support the religious capital claim. That would be circular reasoning.

The 'Lower Orders' Move

Another popular move is to suggest that these 'ethical atheists' tend to be middle-class, intelligent and well-educated. Perhaps they can get by, morally speaking, without religion. But that's not to say that religion isn't necessary to keep the lower orders in check. The thought that, 'If only we could get those working-class yobs from the council estate down the road to believe in God, perhaps they would stop vandalizing our phone boxes and stealing our cars', has an enduring appeal.

This is a pretty elitist point of view, of course: we can get by without religion; the common rabble can't. Many liberals would no doubt prefer it not to be true. But the truth is not always what we would like it to be. It's not enough to deal with this suggestion simply to condemn it on 'politically correct' grounds or to mount an *ad hominem* attack on those putting it forward – 'You're a bunch of arrogant elitists!' Perhaps those making the claim are elitists. They may still be right.

A better response is to ask, again, *why* we should think the 'lower orders' move is true. What's the evidence?

True, there's evidence that religious belief can have a positive impact on social behaviour. Statistics suggest that US cities with high church membership rates have lower rates of crime, drug and alcohol abuse than those with low membership rates (Stark and

Bainbridge 1997). But that's not yet to say religion is necessary if morality is to survive. It's not to suggest, as Kristol and Strauss do, that without religion, society will, or will probably, fall apart. That's a much stronger claim.

Nor is it to say that, while religion can have a positive effect, other things might not be *even more* effective at combating social disorder. We have seen, for example, that when the kind of Liberal philosophy programme recommended in chapter three has been tested in schools – including, crucially, schools with a high proportion of their intake from the economically disadvantaged – the improvements in terms of self-esteem and social behaviour have been dramatic. So it may be that *philosophy is actually far more potent than religion in this respect.*

In short, the positive evidence that even the common rabble can't get by, or even are unlikely to get by, without religion is weak.

Further Problems with the View that Morality is Causally Dependent Upon Religion

Still more evidence against the view that morality is dependent on religion is provided by Fukuyama (the thinker probably best-known for declaring the 'End of History'). In his paper 'The contours of remoralization', Fukuyama (2004: 108) points out that Asia …

> provides important counter examples to the view that moral order depends on religion … The dominant cultural force in traditional Chinese society was, of course, Confucianism, which is not a religion at all but rather a rational, secular ethical doctrine.
> The history of China is replete with instances of moral decline and moral renewal, but none of these is linked particularly to anything a Westerner would call religion. And it is hard to make the case that levels of ordinary morality are lower in Asia than in parts of the world dominated by transcendental religion.

There's also a growing body of scientific evidence that our morality is, to some degree, a part of our genetic inheritance. In *The Origins of Virtue*, Ridley (1997: 249) explains why science now suggests that 'there was morality before the Church'. Our moral code was, at least in part, written into our genes long before it was written into any religious book. But if that is true, that makes the claim that religion is essential if morality is to survive look even more dubious. True, perhaps these discoveries do not establish that religion is unnecessary: perhaps we need both the right kind of genes *and* the right kind of religious environment to develop into fully moral beings. But these discoveries do dramatically narrow the gap that religion is supposedly required to fill between our nature and our moral behaviour.

But perhaps the most glaring problem with the claim that religion is essential, or very important, to sustain moral, law-abiding behaviour is the fact, already mentioned, that the social disorder experienced by the highly religious US is much more severe than it is in far less religious democracies elsewhere. In a paper published recently in *Journal of Religion and Society*, Paul (2005) reports the results of his cross-national study comparing the various detailed and now-widely available statistics for levels of religiosity, homicide, abortion, sexually transmitted disease (STD), suicide, life expectancy and teen pregnancy across the developed, democratic world. Paul (2005) found that

> [i]n general, higher rates of belief in and worship of a creator correlate with higher rates of homicide, juvenile and early adult mortality, STD infection rates, teen pregnancy, and abortion in the prosperous democracies. The most theistic prosperous democracy, the US, is exceptional, but not in the manner Franklin predicted. The United States is almost always the most dysfunctional of the developed democracies, sometimes spectacularly so, and almost always scores poorly. The view of the US as a 'shining city on the hill' to the rest of the world is falsified when it comes to basic measures of societal health.

Oddly enough, Paul found that it was the *least* religious nations that were *most* successful in limiting social dysfunction. Of course, Paul is not claiming that religion causes social dysfunction. That would be an unwarranted leap of logic. His point is the modest one that these statistics do not support the view that religiosity helps improve social health. In fact they tend to undermine the claim that religion is essential, or even highly important, for society's moral health.

Notice that *neither the 'moral capital' nor the 'lower orders' move is adequate to explain away these statistics*. Both moves spectacularly fail to account for why, if the increase in social disorder experienced by the US over the last half century or so is primarily down to loss of religious belief, that disorder should be so much *greater* in the still highly religious US than it is among the heathens of Western Europe.

A Further Problem

The evidence does not strongly support the view that religion is required, or is even highly important, for a nation's social and moral health. Which is not to say that religion does not have some positive effect, of course. But even if there were overwhelming evidence that religion did have a powerful effect on, say, reducing crime, would that necessarily justify us in using religion to that end?[5]

Here's an analogy. William Bennett, the former US Secretary of State for Education, said recently in an interview that if

> ... you wanted to reduce crime ... if that were your sole purpose, you could abort every black baby in this country, and your crime rate would go down.[6]

Not surprisingly, this comment attracted a great deal of attention. Presumably, Bennett's point is that crime is significantly more likely to be committed by a black person than a white. Let's just suppose – merely for the sake of argument, I should stress – that Bennett is right that aborting black babies would indeed bring the crime rate down (notice, incidentally, that aborting male babies would probably have that effect too, as more crime is committed by men than by women). Would that morally justify us in doing it? Of course not. As Bennett himself points out, aborting all African-American babies 'would be an impossible, ridiculous, and morally reprehensible thing to do' (Kristol 1999: 132–133).

The moral is obvious. Even if we could reduce crime by spreading religious belief, that wouldn't necessarily justify us in doing so. Particularly if, as Leo Strauss claims, religion is a fraud. If religion is a fraud, then it remains debatable, to say the least, whether that fraud should be perpetrated on the public, irrespective of the impact on crime.

Religion and the Liberal Approach

Let's sum up. Many confidently assert that morality cannot, or is unlikely to, survive without religion (Moloney even insists it has to be *Judeo-Christian* religion). But the claim is a 'factoid' – a declaration endlessly repeated in certain circles to the point where everyone just assumes it must be true, without it ever being subjected to much serious critical scrutiny. You need only think about the claim critically for five minutes to see just how very dubious it is. Unfortunately, in some quarters, thinking about it for five minutes is something that rarely gets done. Incessantly repeating the mantra that 'morality depends on religion' is no compensation for not having a decent argument.

But let's suppose for a moment – again, merely for the sake of argument, you understand – that religion is highly desirable, perhaps even essential, for our moral health. What, then, would be the implications of this for the Liberal approach to moral education outlined in chapter three?

At first sight, *there are none*. Even if, for a healthy society, children do need a religious upbringing (which it seems they don't), *a religious upbringing is in any case compatible with a Liberal upbringing*. As this book has repeatedly emphasized, the Liberal approach is consistent with raising children within a religious tradition.

To this the reply may be: 'But a Liberal religious education results in a feeble, watered-down version of the kind of religion we need. In particular, it results in a relativistic, non-judgementalist brand of religion.' We've seen, for example, that Himmelfarb claims a key part of the explanation for America's moral malaise is that its religious belief is tainted by relativism and non-judgementalism.

The religious belief of many Americans may be a mile wide but it's only an inch deep because, thinks Himmelfarb, while they believe in God, they are also wedded to non-judgementalism ('But who am I to judge?') and the kind of relativism on which all moral and religious beliefs are equally 'valid'. 'In order to combat this sort of relativism and non-judgementalism,' it might be argued, 'we need to return to Authority-based methods or moral and religious education.'

But this, too, is untrue. The claim that a Liberal religious education must involve a commitment to relativism is false. In fact we've seen that the kind of Liberal moral education recommended in chapter three looks like it may be our best defence *against* relativism. Again, there's no case here for rejecting a Liberal approach to moral and religious education.

The Last Ditch Argument

To this, the final, last ditch reply may be:

> Very well, suppose I accept that a Liberal approach to moral education is consistent with raising children within a religious tradition. Suppose I concede that your kind of Liberal moral education need not promote non-judgementalism and relativism. Still, if religious belief is false, or at least pretty unreasonable, then, by exposing it to the truth-and-falsity-detecting-power of reason, its falsity or unreasonableness is likely to be laid bare. In which case children won't grow up believing it. We need, then, to make sure that children are thoroughly religiously indoctrinated – that religion is inextricably woven into the fabric of their lives – long before we allow them to start thinking at all critically about it (and perhaps not even then). Only then is their religious belief likely to resist exposure to critical scrutiny. So we must reject the Liberal approach after all. We're going to have to get young people to turn their powers of reason off, at least so far as religion is concerned. If religious belief is indispensable to our moral health, then there's a good pragmatic case for getting the

young to accept religious beliefs on 'faith' from a religious
Authority.

This is a feeble argument premised on a series of dubious 'ifs': if religious belief is false or unreasonable, and if its falsehood/ unreasonableness is likely to be exposed by independent critical thought if individuals aren't religiously indoctrinated early on, and if religious belief is nevertheless indispensable to our moral health, then we should religiously indoctrinate the young and discourage them from thinking too carefully or critically about what they're told to believe.

We've already seen that the final 'if' looks particularly suspect. Kristol (who may not endorse this argument, by the way) attempts to justify it by insisting that the alternative to religion – what he calls 'secular rationalism' – cannot provide a rational foundation for morality (like MacIntyre and Gray, Kristol thinks the 'Enlightenment project' had to fail – he says 'Philosophy can analyse moral codes in interesting ways, but it cannot create them' (1999: 132–3)).[7] But of course, even if Kristol is right and 'secular rationalism' can't provide a rational foundation for morality, *neither can religion, particularly if, as another premise of the last ditch argument actually requires, religion is itself false or at least unreasonable. So, if the failure to provide a rational foundation for morality must lead us to reject 'secular humanism', shouldn't it lead us to reject religion too?*

The answer to this, presumably, is that the common herd at least need the *illusion* of a firm moral foundation that religion offers. They need that psychological crutch. But we've already seen that the claim that religion is psychologically required to keep the majority of us on an even moral keel is not well supported by the empirical evidence. In fact the evidence tends to undermine it.

So even this last ditch attempt to discredit the Liberal approach to religious education turns out to be a flop.

Conclusion and Recommendation
Thirteen

This book has two key conclusions. The first conclusion is that there are powerful arguments for embracing a highly Liberal approach to moral and religious education – an approach that emphasizes the importance of encouraging independent critical thought and judgement rather than more-or-less uncritical deference to Authority. These arguments include the following:

1. There's growing evidence that the kind of philosophical, Liberal moral education outlined in chapter three brings lasting, measurable educational benefits, including increased intelligence and emotional and social maturity.
2. A healthy democracy needs to raise new citizens to think and judge independently. It needs to ensure they have the intellectual, social and emotional maturity to exercise their democratic responsibilities properly, so that they are not easily psychologically manipulated. Unlike more Authority-based approaches, the Liberal approach fosters these skills and helps develop that kind of maturity.
3. There's evidence that such a Liberal education also provides an important defence against a certain kind of moral catastrophe seen repeatedly in the twentieth century (in places like Nazi Germany, Russia, Cambodia and China). It can also help immunize new citizens against the wiles of religious cults and other forms of psychological manipulation and brainwashing. There's a strong case for including it in any educational

strategy designed to frustrate those intent on turning young Muslims into weapons of jihad.

4. Rather than spreading relativism and non-judgementalism, this kind of Liberal approach actually provides us with a potent weapon to wield *against* relativism.

5. In any case we *cannot* do what those at the Authoritarian end of the Liberal/Authoritarian scale encourage individuals to do: to hand over responsibility for making moral judgements to some external Authority. Like it or not, the responsibility for making moral judgements has a boomerang-like quality – it always comes back to you.

The second conclusion is that the case *against* the Liberal approach is remarkably feeble. There really is no good argument for moving back in the direction of Authority-based moral and religious education. This is not an issue for compromise – those who continue to condemn all Liberals as relativists and insist we need to rehabilitate Authority with a capital 'A' need to have explained to them, clearly and forcefully, why their arguments are confused. It's particularly important *the myth that our options are either relativism or Authoritarianism should no longer go largely unchallenged*. The public needs reminding that there are other, better, options.

Recommendations Regarding Religious and Moral Education

Given the strength of the case for Liberal moral and religious education, let's finish by considering a concrete recommendation. The British Prime Minister is keen on faith schools and is seeking to increase their number. One hundred and fifty new Islamic schools are already in the pipeline and more are on the way. New Sikh and Hindu schools will also be built. This book does not argue against faith schools. But it does argue against Authority-based religious schooling. Given the strength of the case for the Liberal approach, is there not a good case for ensuring that *every* school, state-funded or not, should do the following?

1. *Have a syllabus that includes periods in which open, philosophical discussion of important moral, cultural, political and religious question takes place.* These sessions should be run by educators with some training in running a philosophical discussion. Safeguards should be put in place to ensure that pupils are not subtly (or not-so-subtly) psychologically pressured into not asking certain sorts of question or making certain sorts of point (e.g. about religion).

2. *Present their pupils with a broad range of different political, moral and religious beliefs and arguments.* It's important alternative points of view are not caricatured or demolished as mere straw men. One way to avoid this is to allow pupils to hear these alternative points of view from those that hold them. Students should get at least some chance actively to engage in discussion with those from other faiths. And also, I should stress, with those of no faith. While many religious schools have few qualms about exposing their pupils to those from other faiths, they often get very nervous indeed about handing them over to an atheist for half an hour (as I know from personal experience).

3. *Where religious education is given, include at least some basic philosophy of religion.* This should include some discussion of the classic arguments both for *and against* the existence of God. Any child that leaves school having received a 'religious education' in which all objections to their faith have been airbrushed out has, in truth, been indoctrinated, not educated.

Lots of educators, including many religious educators, will be comfortable with these suggestions. Plenty of religious schools already educate in accordance with at least some of them. But of course, many will reject them. In fact the suggestion that all schools be *compelled* to accept them is likely to provoke outrage in some quarters. Some will wheel out the kind of objections we've already examined. In particular, you can be sure someone will insist this is merely a proposal to indoctrinate children with relativism.

Here's one final illustration of this sort of attack on the Liberal approach. In 2004, the UK's Institute for Public Policy Research

(IPPR) proposed that all children should be exposed to a range of religious faiths and atheism, and also that they be taught to think critically about religious belief. The IPPR recommended that

> [c]hildren with strong religious beliefs would be encouraged to question them and to ask what grounds there are for holding them ... Pupils would be actively encouraged to question the religious beliefs they bring with them into the classroom ...[1]

Some Christians were happy with this. Chris Curtis, director of the Luton Churches Education Trust, said:

> Christianity stands head and shoulders above the rest ... therefore I'm not afraid. I want young people to understand the different varieties of faith and choose the Christian faith by informed choice, rather than because it's the only thing they came across.[2]

That's an admirably Liberal attitude. But not everyone was quite so enthusiastic about the recommendation. Melanie Phillips's response to the IPPR's Liberal suggestion was to quote approvingly from a *Daily Telegraph* editorial:

> As [this] Telegraph leader comments, this is nothing other than yet another attempt at ideological indoctrination: 'It reflects the belief that parents who pass on the Christian faith are guilty of indoctrinating their children, and that it is the role of the state to stop them. The IPPR and its allies in the Government are not so much interested in promoting diversity as in replacing one set of orthodoxies by another: the joyless ideology of cultural relativism.'[3]

Why both Phillips and the *Daily Telegraph* are pretty confused should now, I hope, be clear.

To begin with, notice that Phillips claims that to get children to think critically and independently about religion is itself 'ideological indoctrination' (amazingly, the *Telegraph* even calls it 'authoritarian' (2004)). That's false. To encourage children to think critically and independently is not to indoctrinate them – in fact we've seen that it's their best defence against being indoctrinated.

Undoubtedly, the IPPR is concerned that some religious parents are guilty of indoctrinating their children into mindless uncritical acceptance. But that's a sensible concern, for the reasons explained in this book. The IPPR does not argue against religious education *per se*. It merely emphasizes the importance of a Liberal, critical dimension to that education. And what is the problem with that?

'Relativism! You're spreading relativism!' comes the reply. But to encourage critical thought about religion is *not* to promote relativism. It's one of our best defences against it, in fact.

Parental Freedom

Still, there's one important objection to the suggestion that all schools be compelled to meet these minimum standards that we've not yet addressed. The objection concerns parental freedom. Let's finish by taking a closer look at it.

Surely, as a parent, I have a right to send my child to a school that will raise her in accordance with my own religious convictions. Surely, if I believe it's in her best interests that she not be encouraged to think critically about her own religious tradition, that she mix only, or almost only, with children of the same faith, and that she not be exposed to other points of view (I feel they will only 'corrupt' her), then that is my right. The government has no business stopping me.

Of course, we can concede to the proponent of this objection that the state should respect parental freedom as much as it reasonably can. But there are limits. If a practice is physically or psychologically stunting children, surely we are justified in banning it.

Take foot-binding. For almost a thousand years, the Chinese considered it desirable that women have very small feet. The 'ideal' foot was only three-to-four inches long. Most parents would bind the feet of their daughters, forcing them into ever-smaller pairs of shoes in order to make their feet tiny. As a result, many women were left incapable even of standing on their own two feet, let alone running or jumping. Were this practice now to spring up in the UK, it would rightly be banned. Yes we should respect parental wishes.

But there are limits. Parents should not be allowed permanently to physically stunt or damage their children.

But if parents should be stopped from stunting their children's physical development, shouldn't they be prohibited from stunting their psychological development too? Surely we're as justified in preventing parents binding children's minds as we are in preventing them binding children's feet? If children are going to end up intellectually, emotionally and socially damaged as a result of being 'educated' in the way their parents demand – if the result will be new citizens *psychologically* incapable of standing properly on their own two feet – shouldn't we take steps? Isn't it important we act to maintain a healthy democracy?

A System of Political Schools

If you're not persuaded by that, then consider another analogy. Suppose that, across the UK, private *political* schools began to appear. A neoconservative school opens in Billericay, followed by a communist school in Middlesbrough. Before you know it, there are hundreds of these schools across the country, of every political hue.

This would increase 'choice' for parents, of course. Parents with strong political convictions would now have the option of sending their children to the political school of their choosing.

Suppose these new schools discriminate against pupils of other political persuasions. If you're a socialist, you're probably going to find it hard to get little Sophie into Neocon High. Only communists are welcome at Trotsky Towers.

Political education at these schools largely takes the form of indoctrination. Portraits of their political leaders beam beatifically down from classroom walls. Each day begins with the collective singing of a political anthem. Pupils are never encouraged to think critically and independently about political questions. They are expected to defer more-or-less unquestioningly to their school's Authority and its revered political texts. Only ideas approved by the school's political Authority are taught. Children are never exposed to alternative political points of view (except, perhaps, in a rather caricatured form, so that they can be all the more sweepingly dismissed).

If such schools did start popping up, there would no doubt be outrage. The public would rightly feel that 'political education' had taken an unacceptably sinister turn. 'This is not political *education*,' they would say. 'These schools are educationally *stunting* children, forcing their minds into political-approved moulds.' They would be right. These are the kind of schools you find in totalitarian political regimes – in places like Stalinist Russia or North Korea. They're the kind of chillingly Orwellian schools Westerners typically hold up as prime examples of how *not* to raise good citizens. There's a powerful case for saying that, if they are to remain healthy, democracies can't afford to tolerate this sort of 'education'.

Faced with the rise of such schools, the public would surely demand that the government act. I'd guess the bare minimum they'd require would be that the government ensure both that all children are allowed to think freely and critically, and that they are exposed to a wide range of political points of view.

Now the question, of course, is this: if we're justified in restricting parental freedom when it comes to Authoritarian political schools, *why aren't we justified in restricting it when it comes to their religious equivalents?* If we're justified in denying parents the right to send their children to schools like Trotsky Towers and Neocon High, *then why not to an equally Authoritarian Muslim, Jewish or Catholic school?*[4]

Parental freedom is surely a very dubious justification for allowing such Authoritarian schools to continue, be they political or religious.

Dealing with a Reply

In reply to this, a defender of Authoritarian religious schooling may insist that political points of view are somehow special – unlike religious points of view, *they* are not something young people should be expected to accept uncritically.

But this is to overlook the fact that *many religious points of view are also political.* Clearly, religious points of view on homosexuality, a woman's place in the home, abortion, the State of Israel, jihad, and even poverty and injustice, are all *intensely* political. In fact, there are few aspects of religious belief that don't have an important political dimension. So a blanket prohibition on Authoritarian political teaching couldn't help but be a prohibition on a great deal of Authoritarian religious teaching as well.

And yet, as I say, Authoritarian religious teaching is something that many of those who consider Authoritarian political schools utterly beyond the pale nevertheless feel pretty comfortable with. Authoritarian religious schooling is considered by many to be not just tolerable but, in some cases, even highly desirable. My question is: *why* does the addition of a religious dimension to what is taught suddenly legitimate the adoption of an Authoritarian approach? *Why* does the fact that they happen to be religious beliefs mean that the parents' desire for an Authoritarian education should now be respected?

These are not easy questions to answer.

A final thought. One reason, I suspect, why many of us who find Authoritarian political schools chillingly Orwellian remain comfortable with their religious equivalents is *inertia*. Authoritarian political schools would be a shocking new development. But there have always been Authoritarian religious schools. Familiarity, and perhaps a sense of inevitability, has blunted the sense of shock and outrage we might otherwise feel. But this is hardly a justification for allowing such schools to continue. Nor is it to say that we *shouldn't* find their continued existence pretty shocking.

The time, surely, has come to draw a line under Authority-based moral and religious education.

Appendix one

Some may remain unsatisfied with my rejection of the suggestion that the Enlightenment – or more specifically, Kantian Enlightenment (which is, of course, what's being defended here) – is somehow to blame for the Holocaust.

It might be pointed out, for example, that while Hitler's and Stalin's murderous regimes were indeed profoundly anti-Liberal, that doesn't establish that they weren't the *end product* of the Enlightenment and Liberal values. The Enlightenment might still have been causally involved in producing these horrors. Just as an overly generous parent can produce a selfish child, so the rise of highly Liberal ideas might produce, in reaction, a highly Authoritarian result.

Clearly there are causal connections between the Enlightenment and both these horrendous episodes in our recent history. The Enlightenment was a hugely pivotal period. If there had been no Enlightenment, then the history of the twentieth century would have no doubt been very different. Perhaps there would have been no Holocaust and no Gulag (though there might have been something just as bad, of course). But to point out this possible, even probable, causal connection is *not* to establish that the philosophical ideas of the Enlightenment are to blame for the Holocaust and the Gulag.

After all, if there had been no Jesus, then there would have been no Christian religion, and thus no Holy Inquisition. There's a similar causal dependence. That doesn't establish that Jesus' philosophy is to *blame* for the horrors of the Inquisition. Jesus would no doubt have been profoundly opposed to the Inquisition, just as Kant would have been profoundly opposed to the Holocaust.

In reply, it might be said that while the ideas of Jesus did not make the Inquisition inevitable, *the ideas of the Enlightenment did make something like the Holocaust inevitable*. We saw back in chapter one that philosophers such as Alisdair MacIntyre and John Gray have argued that a key project of the Enlightenment was that of providing morality with a wholly rational, tradition-free foundation. They also argue that this project had inevitably to fail. But if it had to fail, leaving morality without *any* foundation (and wasn't that Nietzsche's insight?), wasn't it inevitable that morality would then collapse? So (some might conclude) the Enlightenment did after all make it inevitable that the West would drift into nihilism and, ultimately, moral catastrophe. So the ideas of the Enlightenment are ultimately to blame for the Holocaust.

Of course, this explanation of the Holocaust doesn't fit terrifically well with Hitler's earlier professed Christianity. There's no evidence Hitler was ever a moral nihilist. Quite the contrary (remember Hitler's emphasis on the importance of religious schools to provide a firm moral foundation). But even if the above explanation were correct, it would still fail to discredit the Liberal approach to moral education defended here. For *the claim that morality can be given a wholly rational, tradition-free foundation is not something that Liberalism-with-a-capital-'L', or any of the arguments for Liberalism offered here, require.* As is explained in more detail in chapter nine, to agree with Kant that it's a good idea to get individuals to think for themselves about right and wrong and apply their own powers of reason rather than defer to some external Authority is *not* to assume that reason *alone* can determine right and wrong for us. We can safely jettison that dubious Enlightenment assumption while still insisting on the importance of autonomous critical thought.

The evidence suggests that our best protection against such moral catastrophes is not to raise new citizens to be deferential to religious Authority, but to raise them to be clear-headed, independent critical thinkers who have been encouraged to examine their own beliefs and to look at things from other points of view.

Lyotard

One philosopher well-known for suggesting that the Enlightenment was responsible for Auschwitz is the post-modernist Jean-Francois Lyotard. Lyotard believed the Enlightenment 'grand narrative' involved the thought that human beings should be treated as just one more part of nature to be rationally mastered, and that once reason was applied in this way, progress would be inevitable. Auschwitz is a symbol of the failure of this 'grand narrative' and in fact a result of it (see, for example, Lyotard 1992: 30–32). This is all pretty tendentious. But, in any case, even if it were true, let's again remind ourselves that the Liberal, Kantian position on the importance of getting individuals to think critically and independently rather than defer to Authority does not require that we sign up to any such 'grand narrative'. In fact, an approach to moral education that engages the individual's own powers of reason is surely one of the best ways of avoiding treating humans as just more 'bits of nature'. Unlike approaches to moral education based on psychological manipulation of the sort we saw in chapter four (approaches which do indeed treat subjects as just one more part of the causally-manipulable natural order) a Liberal approach engages the subject's own power of reason, puts pupil and teacher on a level playing field, so that the pupil may actually succeed in showing that it is the teacher who is wrong.

Incidentally, Kant himself is very clear that treating others as rational agents involves treating them as ends in themselves rather than as means to an end – that's to say, it requires that we not treat them instrumentally. Odd, then, that Kant and his Enlightenment followers should be accused of promoting the exact opposite view.

Many 'post-moderns' dismiss reason as just another form of coercive, Authoritarian thought-control. But the kind of 'compulsion' residing in rational argument is not just another form of causal compulsion. It doesn't determine what you will believe (in the way that, say, psychological manipulation, brain-washing or a totalitarian regime tries to do), it merely shows what you ought to believe if you want to give your beliefs the best chance of being true. Unfortunately, this distinction between the causal 'must' and the logical 'must' is lost on those critics of Enlightenment who maintain that the use of reason is just another form of Authoritarian bullying.

One reason why this distinction gets overlooked is that often, when reason is applied, various other things are going on as well – various psychological factors may also play a causal role in determining what we believe – factors that have little or anything to with the truth of the belief in question. I might think I have been persuaded by rational argument, but maybe I have simply caved into peer pressure, or capitulated to my desire to conform. Still, even while we may flatter ourselves about what extent we are rational, it doesn't follow that reason has no power to lead us to the truth, nor that it's not our best defence against our being psychologically manipulated and misled in this way.

Christian Resistance to the Nazis

Defenders of Authority-based values education sometimes point out that Christians and other religious believers have often been at the vanguard in the fight against totalitarian regimes, as if this somehow justified a more Authority-based approach to moral and religious education. But of course it doesn't. The Liberal approach is, to repeat, compatible with both a Christian upbringing and Christian moral values.

Moreover, if Glover and the Oliners are right, it was those Christians raised in a Liberal, Enlightened way, who had been raised not to just follow Authority, who were most likely to resist the 'final solution'. As the Oliners point out, religiosity *per se* 'was only weakly related to rescue'.

The Eichmann Case

Another point often made in an attempt to shift at least some of the blame for the Holocaust onto the Enlightenment is that Germany in the 1920s and 1930s was heavily steeped in the philosophy of Kant. Some defenders of Authority-based values education like to point out that, according to Arendt (1994: 135), witness to the trial of the mass-murdering Nazi Eichmann, Eichmann described himself as having 'lived his whole life according to Kant's moral precepts'. Is this not a powerful indictment of Kant's Enlightenment vision?

No. Arendt (1994: 136, emphasis added) goes on to say that Eichmann's claim is 'outrageous, on the face of it, and also incomprehensible, since Kant's moral philosophy is so closely bound up with man's faculty of judgement, which *rules out* blind obedience'. Eichmann may indeed have been familiar with Kant's ethics. That doesn't mean Eichmann followed Kant's advice. Arendt (1994: 136) says that 'from the moment he was charged with carrying out the final solution he had ceased to live according to Kantian principles'.

That Eichmann seriously misunderstood Kant was made clear when he said that Kant's categorical imperative could be summarized as, 'Be loyal to the laws, be a disciplined person, live an orderly life, do not come into conflict with laws'.[1] It's perfectly clear that Kant's notion of duty is *not* equivalent to following orders, obey the law, etc. Ironically, Eichmann thought Kant's philosophy was that the individual should uncritically accept and follow the instructions of Authority: *Eichmann thought Kant was an Authoritarian*.

Eichmann certainly wasn't what Kant would call Enlightened. Nor does there appear to be any evidence that Eichmann was raised in a Liberal way, encouraged and trained to question and think, to take individual responsibility rather than defer to Authority. Contrary to what some Authoritarians have suggested, Eichmann's behaviour cannot fairly be blamed on Kant or the Enlightenment. In fact, it would be more accurate to blame it on his Authoritarian mind-set.

An anonymous reviewer of the proposal for this book questioned the suggestion that an Enlightened approach to moral education might provide us with a defence against this kind of moral catastrophe, maintaining that 'no culture was more drenched in Kantianism than Germany in the 1930s'. Perhaps Kant's philosophy was widely known in Germany in the 1930s. But were his highly Liberal views on moral autonomy and Enlightenment? In Eichmann's case, the answer is clearly 'no'.

Appendix two

In chapter eleven we saw that two points made by MacIntyre – that morality cannot be given a wholly rational foundation and that reason is inevitably rooted in a tradition – are in fact compatible with the Liberal idea that we should reject Authority-based approaches to moral education and instead encourage an open, questioning and critical attitude in our pupils.

But none of this is yet to say that MacIntyre himself is mistaken about anything. MacIntyre uses these points to attack what he calls 'the Enlightenment project', by which he means the project of providing a 'rational foundation for and justification of morality' (MacIntyre 1985: 43). The points made by MacIntyre certainly count heavily against 'Enlightenment' as MacIntyre characterizes it. But they do not count against 'Enlightenment' as Kant characterizes – which, as I explained in chapter one, is the variety of Enlightenment defended in this book.

MacIntyre's work is subtle and deserves more attention than can be given here. But it is not clear to me to what extent MacIntyre himself would wish to reject Enlightenment as Kant characterizes it. Moreover, while MacIntyre is critical of 'liberalism', it's not obvious to me to what extent he intends to be critical of Liberalism with a capital 'L'.

MacIntyre (1985: 222) does say that all reasoning takes place within the context of some traditional mode of thought. But he doesn't think this means that certain traditional ways of thinking must therefore be protected from rational scrutiny – in fact he clearly states 'nothing can claim exemption from reflective critique' (MacIntyre 1994: 289; emphasis added). MacIntyre (1994) does say 'well-founded reflective critique can never be disengaged from those contexts of practice from which it acquires its point and purpose' and that 'Rational enquiry is essentially social' (MacIntyre 1999: 156) – rational enquiry cannot be engaged in a tradition-free way by a wholly socially-disengaged individual. But that's not to say that we should encourage anyone – even the young – to *avoid* engaging in it. MacIntyre (1985: 222) says 'when a tradition is in good order it is always partially constituted by an argument about the goods the pursuit of which give that tradition its particular point and purpose. Traditions, when vital, embody continuities of conflict.' MacIntyre thinks conflicts and argument over fundamentals is actually a good, healthy thing for a tradition. It seems, then, that while MacIntyre wants us to be aware of the limitations of reason, he still considers reason a powerful tool, a tool that not only *can* be applied, but *should* be applied, even to a tradition's most fundamental beliefs and practices.

But then, *far from rejecting Enlightenment as Kant characterizes, it looks as if MacIntyre may actually be a fan.* MacIntyre believes we can and should think carefully and critically, even about the most fundamental beliefs and practices of our own tradition (while still acknowledging, of course, that there is no wholly tradition-free way of doing this). Nothing should simply be accepted on the say so of Authority. Nothing should be placed beyond critical scrutiny.

Of course, this still leaves open to what extent *children* should be allowed or even encouraged to think carefully and critically about fundamentals. MacIntyre does say that to master a practice requires acceptance of authority and that traditions have 'an authority' (MacIntyre 1985: 190). But what exactly does 'authority' mean here? Does it mean Authority-with-a-capital-'A'? Is it an Authority to which we must unquestioningly, uncritically defer, at least in the earliest stages of our immersion in the practice? That is not clear.

We have seen that for Aristotle, for example, becoming good involves acquiring certain skills, entering into certain practices.

This requires discipline and the application of authority with a small 'a': children must be got into the habit of doing good, so that that they become good. But there seems no obvious reason why the application of 'authority' in this sense shouldn't be compatible with autonomous critical reflection from a young age. Certainly there's no case here for *suppressing* such reflection (which is what Sacks seems to want).

Indeed, if critical reflection on moral fundamentals is, as MacIntyre claims, essential for a healthy tradition – part of the life-blood of that tradition – and if 'nothing can claim exemption from reflective critique', then surely we need to be trained to do it well. So, while MacIntyre does speak approvingly of 'authority' (and attacks 'liberal individualism'), it is not at all clear that he wants to see any sort of return to Authority with a capital 'A'.

And yet MacIntyre has become the pin-up boy of many Authoritarians. His arguments are regularly co-opted to justify a return to Authority-based moral and religious education.

Having said that, there is at least one passage in *After Virtue* in which MacIntyre might *seem* to be attacking the Kantian vision of the individual as 'sovereign in his moral authority'. Some might interpret the following as arguing that Kant's Enlightenment vision results in morality appearing to be nothing more than a matter of mere subjective choice and preference.

> On the one hand the individual moral agent, freed from hierarchy and teleology, conceives of himself and is conceived of by moral philosophers as sovereign in his moral authority. On the other hand the inherited, if partially transformed rules of morality have to be found some new status, deprived as they have been of their older teleological character and their even more ancient categorical character as expressions of divine law. If such rules cannot be found some new status which will make appeal to them rational, appeal to them will indeed appear as a mere instrument of individual desire and will (MacIntyre 1985: 62).

A closer look at this passage reveals, though, that its Kant's vision *combined with the loss of the old teleological and religious dimension to our moral thinking* that MacIntyre thinks results in moral rules appearing to be nothing more than 'instruments of individual desire and will'.

My question is: is Kant's vision of the morally autonomous individual itself contributing to this impression of morality as being nothing more than an expression of personal preference, or *is it the loss of the teleological and religious dimensions alone that's generating that appearance?*

After all, if we lose the teleological and religious dimension, but also reject Kant's vision and instead embrace some external Authority-with-a-capital-A, morality will *still* appear as a mere 'instrument of individual desire or will.' *Only now it will appear as the instrument of the desire or will of that external Authority.* What MacIntyre has discredited, perhaps, is the idea that we can do without the religiously-rooted teleology. Kant's vision is not yet undermined.

Why can't we have a religious, teleological conception of morality (which I am not rejecting here, of course – by all means argue that we need to bring it back) while also rejecting Authority-with-a-capital-A and embracing instead Kant's vision of the morally autonomous individual who must think for him- or herself? Why *must* the Liberal attitude inevitably result in moral rules appearing to be nothing more than expressions of personal preference? I don't yet see why it must. Nor is it clear that MacIntyre thinks it must.

Notes

Introduction

1. *Gallup, Daily Telegraph*, 5 July 1996.
2. When Bob Dole accused Bill Clinton of being a 'closet liberal' in the 1996 presidential election, Clinton strongly denied it. As Drury (1997: 171) says, 'it was clear by then that anyone who wanted to be a liberal had better keep it a secret'.

Chapter One

1. Indeed, an anonymous reviewer of the proposal for this book suggested that few intellectual historians now consider Kant an Enlightenment philosopher. On the other hand, the *Oxford Companion to Philosophy* ranks Kant as 'one of the last, and one of the greatest, Enlightenment thinkers' (see entry on 'Enlightenment').
2. Perhaps the most important 'Enlightened' Islamic thinker is Averroes (also known as Ibn Rushd), to whom Western Enlightenment owes a great deal (see for example, Mourad Wahba, 'Averroes as a Bridge', in THINK, issue 12). Galileo, in particular, appears to have been influenced by Averroes. Even today in Iran – a highly Authoritarian state – many clerics are surprisingly Enlightened in their views. For those interested in finding out more, I highly recommend Jahanpour (forthcoming).
3. For a critical discussion of young-Earth creationist claims and arguments, see 'Is Creationism Scientific?' in my book *The Philosophy Gym* (Law 2004).

Chapter Two

1. See Phillips (1998) for numerous examples. Phillips is examined in more detail in chapter 8.

2. Pope Benedict (2005) recently warned of the dangers of allowing people to discover their own religious routes:

> If it is pushed too far, religion becomes almost a consumer product ... People choose what they like, and some are even able to make a profit from it. But religion constructed on a 'do-it-yourself' basis cannot ultimately help us.

The suggestion here seems to be that Catholics are obliged to accept whatever they are told to believe, rather than make their own private judgement. Those who dare to make their own judgement are often dismissed by religious conservatives as 'cafeteria Catholics' or 'pick-n-mix Christians'.

3. The Pope, by the way, is not supposed to be infallible about *everything* (I'm sure he's occasionally mistaken about e.g. where he's left his slippers) but only those things on which he pronounces *ex Cathedra*.

Chapter Three

1. The last execution for heresy was in Spain, on July 26th, 1826. Schoolmaster Cayetano Ripoll was a deist (deists believe in God, but think that reason, rather than tradition and revelation, should be the basis of belief). For daring to hold such un-Catholic views, Ripoll was condemned to be hanged (his last words were 'I die reconciled to God and man'). See Kamen (1997: 302) and also Lea (1906–07).

2. Anderson (1995) favours the use of stigmatization as a social tool – he is one of many who recommend ridicule, ostracism, etc. as methods of social control. One of the contributors to *This Will Hurt* even recommends we return to stigmatizing children born out of wedlock. Himmelfarb (1999: 38) (who, incidentally, wrote an approving preface to *This Will Hurt*) also speaks about the importance of stigmatization.

3. I don't deny that rote learning has its place, of course, e.g. learning your timestables. The objection is to the application of rote learning as an alternative to, or in tandem with the suppression of, any free, independent thought. The two are obviously compatible – someone who learns their tables by rote need not be dissuaded from applying their own intelligence and engaging in an open enquiry into e.g. whether and/or why these tables are correct.

4. James Park, director of Antidote, made this point in a talk at the 'Hearts and Minds' Conference jointly organized by Antidote and Sapere at the NUT headquarters in London on 16 November 2005. The classic text in the field of emotional intelligence is of course Goleman's (1996) *Emotional Intelligence*.

5. As many, including the philosopher John Dewey (1897), have stressed. The approach to moral education recommended here is broadly congruent with that advocated by Dewey (although I am by no means offering a blanket endorsement of Dewey). Dewey rejects Authority-based approaches and emphasizes the importance of the social dimension. Dewey says, for example:

> I believe that much of present education fails because it neglects this fundamental principle of the school as a form of community life. It conceives the school as a place where certain information is to be given, where certain lessons are to be learned, or where certain habits are to be formed. The value of these is conceived as lying largely in the remote future; the child must do these things for the sake of something else he is to do; they are mere preparation. As a result they do not become a part of the life experience of the child and so are not truly educative. I believe that the moral education centres upon this conception of the school as a mode of social life, that the best and deepest moral training is precisely that which one gets through having to enter into proper relations with others in a unity of work and thought. The present educational systems, so far as they destroy or neglect this unity, render it difficult or impossible to get any genuine, regular moral training (Dewey).

6. Are most teachers actually trained and equipped to teach children to think cogently, clearly and independently? The answer, in many cases, is clearly 'no'. The kind of skills needed to teach critical thinking and to run an effective class-room 'community of inquiry' are fairly specialist skills in which teachers currently receive little if any formal instruction. If this kind of programme is to be effective, there is no doubt that those running it will need some training (though we shouldn't allow opponents of philosophy in the classroom to exaggerate how much is required – in the highly successful Clackmannanshire programme discussed below, teachers received just two days' training). Without trained educators and facilitators, there's a risk that philosophy in the classroom can degenerate into flaccid exercises in self-expression in which pupils do little more than collectively dive into a stream of consciousness lacking any kind of rigour or structure. Obviously, that's to be avoided.

7. Of course, Liberals can admit it's not *always* appropriate to get into a moral debate, even with older children. They believe only that it is important that there be some space for these kinds of issues to be discussed. I'm not recommending interminable debate wherever and whenever the child might happen to feel like it. Again, that would be a caricature of what's suggested here.

8. From private correspondence with Paul Cleghorn. The preceding information in this paragraph comes from: http://www.aude-education.co.uk/others.htm.

9. I'm referring to the *Northumberland Raising Aspirations In Society* (NRAIS) project, for which a study was recently completed. The results are documented in *Summary of Research Evidence Supporting Philosophy for Children* by Will Ord, Chair of SAPERE, shortly available from SAPERE. Also see www.nrais.org.

10. When I speak of 'children', I'm obviously painting with a broad brush. There may be developmental stages through which children pass that must be taken into account when tailoring this sort of education to their needs. The psychologist Lawrence Kohlberg, for example, has argued that children pass through six clearly definable stages in their moral development – what is appropriate at one stage may be unsuitable at another. However, even Kohlberg claims that what enables children to pass from one stage to the next is intellectual activity – discussion and debate based around moral dilemmas. Whether or not Kohlberg is right, his findings are consistent with what's recommended here. For a good overview of Kohlberg see Crain (1985: 118–136).

11. For further evidence see Trickey and Topping (2004). Also see e.g. Ofsted reports for schools participating in philosophy for children projects summarized in the document *Extracts from Ofsted Inspection Reports Highlighting the Use of Philosophy*, available from SAPERE.

Chapter Four

1. Incidentally, De Tocqueville once said, 'I know of no country in which, speaking generally, there is less independence of mind and true freedom of discussion than in America.' *Democracy in America*, chapter 15, available on-line at http://www.marxists.org/reference/archive/de-tocqueville/democracy-america/ch15.htm.

2. Of course, Mill recognized there are *some* situations in which freedom of speech should be curtailed. Someone who is mischievously about to shout 'fire' in a crowded cinema should clearly be silenced. Mill even says that the opinion that 'corn dealers are starvers of the poor ... ought to be unmolested when simply circulated through the press, but may justly incur punishment when delivered to an excited mob assembled before the house of a corn-dealer, or when handed out among the same mob in the form of a placard' (Himmelfarb 1985). But these are exceptional circumstances in which the result of allowing free speech will very likely be death or serious harm. Society should otherwise allow freedom of thought and expression – including thought and expression about moral and religious matters.

3. Milgram's findings are reported in Milgram (1963). Another famous psychological experiment, performed by Asch (1951), also demonstrates this

sheep-like tendency. Asch showed just how powerful is our tendency to conform, not to authority, but to our peers. Individuals were asked to judge which of two lines was longer (the answer was obvious) after hearing other subjects consistently give the wrong answer. The majority of subjects agreed with the judgement of the bogus majority and gave the wrong answer, despite the evidence of their own senses.

4. Not the *only* cause, of course. See for example the draft report 'Young Muslims and Extremism', commissioned by the British Government, which identifies a number of factors. Available online at: http://www.globalsecurity.org/security/library/report/2004/muslimext-uk.htm#remit.

5. Source: http://thc.worldarcstudio.com/classroom_20040211_JB/gcse/polpot.htm.

6. I recommend a visit to www.chinese-memorial.org for a moving account of exactly who was targeted and why.

Chapter Five

1. Richard Norman emphasized this point to me – and it does explain why the responsibility for making a moral judgement can't be avoided. However, I should add that the point doesn't yet fully explain why the suicide bomber is properly morally *to blame* for what she did. Perhaps she did *have* to make a moral judgement. It doesn't yet follow that she is in any way to blame. After all, I might find myself in a situation where I am forced to make a technical judgement about something of which I know next to nothing. For example, I might be faced with two wires connected to a bomb that is about to explode on board a plane. I know that cutting one wire will save the plane. But, being ignorant about how bombs work, I have no idea which one. So I cut a wire. It's the wrong one. Many die. Am I to blame? No. I *had* to make a technical judgement, but being (quite understandably) technically incompetent in this area, I can be entirely forgiven for making the wrong judgement. But then the fact that the suicide bomber also *has* to make a moral judgement as to whether to follow the advice to blow up a busy supermarket doesn't yet fully explain why she is morally culpable and to blame for making the wrong judgement. To properly explain that, it seems we must *also* acknowledge that (unlike me and my knowledge of bomb disposal) *she should have known better*. What this case brings out is that we suppose that (setting aside cases of brainwashing, the mentally impaired, etc.) *mature human beings have a level of moral competency that works independently of any external authority.*

2. Usually when we do accept a moral expert's advice that should only be because we have ourselves come to recognize why they are correct. That's not typically

the reason why we're justified in trusting the advice of other kinds of expert: doctors, plumbers, lawyers, car mechanics and so on. When you follow a doctor's advice and take a particular pill, it's rarely because the doctor has fully explained to you the science behind her judgement and so convinced you that her advice is good. It doesn't matter if you haven't got the slightest clue why she thinks the pill will work. You can rightly place your 'faith' in her judgement. You can simply take her word for it. You're justified in doing so because she's an acknowledged expert.

The situation is rather different when it comes to moral expertise. Accepting the moral advice of another – even if they are supposedly 'expert' – is *typically* only justified if *you yourself* have come to recognize why they are correct.

I say 'typically', because there may be one or two exceptions to the rule that you should never blindly accept and act on the moral advice of another.

Suppose, for example, that I'm faced with a tough moral dilemma: a dilemma in which a choice must be made, and both choices have serious consequences. And suppose I find I'm just not smart enough to work out which choice is morally justified. I might go to someone whom I have previously established is a good moral judge for their advice. If this person believes the answer is clear, then perhaps I might justifiably follow their advice, even though I am not myself clever enough to follow their justification. However, even in this case, I still have to rely on my own moral judgement in deciding whether or not this other person is, *generally speaking*, a good moral judge. So I still haven't entirely avoided the responsibility for making moral judgements. That responsibility may, *under certain very special circumstances*, such as those just described, be *partially* delegated. It cannot be wholly handed over.

3. Though I should perhaps point out that Kant's own argument for this conclusion is rather different.

4. 'But hang on,' some will reply. 'While you're restricting their behaviour, you are justifying doing so from your own Liberal standpoint. And who's to say that your Liberal standpoint is correct? Maybe it's these Authoritarians who are correct. So you *are*, in effect, imposing your beliefs on them – making them conform to your Liberal sense of what is right and what is wrong.'

Well, yes and no. Again, let's stress that we are restricting their behaviour, *not their freedom of thought and expression*. And why can't this restriction on their behaviour be justified? Surely there are good arguments for supposing that brainwashing and violence are a bad thing. Liberals can give those arguments.

In reply to this, some may say: 'But won't these arguments inevitably just *take* for granted Liberal attitudes? In which case, why, rationally speaking, should the Authoritarians have to accept them? It turns out a Liberal society ultimately cannot rationally justify restricting the behaviour of these Authoritarians in its midst other than in an unacceptably circular way.'

Perhaps there's some truth to this objection. However, the problem, then, is not that Liberals are inconsistent (which is the charge I am dealing with here); it's simply that they can't ultimately rationally justify preventing these Authoritarians from behaving in this sort of way.

Still, if the problem, in the end, is that it's not ultimately possible to provide a rational, non-circular justification for preferring *any* one moral and political system over another (a problem looked at in more detail in chapter nine), be it Liberal or Authoritarian, then it does at least remain true that we haven't been given any reason why we shouldn't prefer a Liberal system unwilling to condone violence and brainwashing to, say, an Authoritarian alternative that does.

Certainly, it remains true to say that we have not uncovered any *inconsistency* in the Liberal position advocated here.

Chapter Six

1. Quoted in *The Observer*, 27 October 1996.
2. Source: http://youthviolence.edschool.virginia.edu/violence-in-schools/national-statistics.html.
3. Source: *Radical Statistics*, issue 83, available online at www.radstats.org.uk/no083/Pennington83.pdf.
4. Source: results of Federal studies summarized at http://www.trinity.edu/~mkearl/fam-type.html.
5. One worry that might be raised about some of these studies is that they compare e.g. rates of offending of children of single parents with those from two-parent families. In order to establish that children who become offenders would have been less likely to offend had their unhappy parents stayed together, the comparison group should be two-parent families that (because of their religious beliefs, social pressure, sense of responsibility to their children, etc.) stayed together despite equally serious marital/relationship problems. It might yet turn out that the children of such unhappy marriages are just as likely to become offenders as those of parents who split.
6. See *Young People and Crime* (Home Office 1995) and Farrington (1995). Both studies are cited by Phillips (1998: 284) in her *All Must Have Prizes*.
7. Quoted by L. M. Bagby at http://www-personal.ksu.edu/~lauriej/links/parallels/aristotle.html.
8. Writing in the *Washington Post* and quoted by C. W. Colson at http://www.airpower.maxwell.af.mil/airchronicles/apj/apj96/sum96/colson.html.
9. Quoted disapprovingly at http://www.slate.com/id/2100437/ and approvingly at http://www.christianitytoday.com/ct/2004/119/42.0.html.

10. Nick Tate speech to the SCAA on 15 January 1996.
11. In 1993, 43 per cent of Americans said that they attended church weekly, compared to 14 per cent in Britain and 12 per cent in France. These statistics are from *The Observer*, 15 February 2004, p. 1. The other statistic is from Himmelfarb (1999: 94–95).

Chapter Eight

1. From the publisher notes on the book's webpage at www.amazon.com.
2. Weblog at http://www.rasmusen.org/w/04.06.13a.htm.
3. Or at least that was what was finally, officially agreed at the Council of Chalcedon in AD 451.
4. As an anonymous reader of this book from a US university reminded me, a similar problem has emerged in the US. Many school districts sign up to the idea that pupils should 'celebrate diversity'. Pupils are told that they must tolerate, and even celebrate, differing religious and cultural points of view. While toleration is clearly to be encouraged, up to a point (Nazis and white supremacists are not usually invited to the 'celebrate diversity' party, and rightly so), if schools tell children they must accept and even celebrate diversity – if they inform children that this is what they *must* believe, and snuff out dissent – then they are themselves guilty of being Authoritarian. Worse still, 'celebrating diversity' can easily degenerate into an orgy of relativism, in which all moral, cultural and religious points of view (except, of course, those not sanctioned by the organizers) are held to be equally 'true'. So *'celebrating diversity' can end up producing a bizarre, muddled-headed mix of Authoritarianism and relativism.*

   As I say, emphasizing the importance of tolerance, and valuing a Liberal culture in which a diverse range of views can be expressed, does not require that we sign up to this 'politically correct' brand of relativism on which all points of view are true. Those insisting that children 'celebrate diversity' need to be much clearer about exactly what it is that they are, and are not, promoting. Unless children gain a clearer, philosophically more sophisticated understanding of what 'celebrating diversity' is about, we run the risk that they'll grow up into 'politically correct' relativists of the most feeble-minded and hypocritical sort.
5. This quotation is taken from http://www.buchanan.org/000-c-culture.html.
6. To be fair to Phillips, she does also say that 'Of course pupils should be taught to think for themselves and should understand the reasoning behind the moral rules they are taught'. But this only makes her attack on Haydon all the more puzzling. For that children should be encouraged to think and question rather than accept uncritically what someone tells them is all Haydon is suggesting in the passage she attacks.

Chapter Nine

1. By the way, the term 'induction' gets used in different ways. I'm using 'induction' quite broadly: I don't just mean it to cover enumerative induction (which is what some people mean by the term). The characterization of induction given here is also intended to cover, e.g. argument to the best explanation.

2. Although there are philosophical arguments (most notably from David Hume) that inductive reasoning is not reasonable. For an outline of Hume's attack on induction, see Law (2003: 152–162).

3. MacIntyre (1959) points out that, actually, 'is' can sometimes entail 'ought' (reprinted in Hudson 1969: 35–50). For example, we suppose, correctly, that the claim that Ted *is* a doctor does entail that he *ought* to behave in certain ways: that he *ought* to attempt to save life where he can, for example. But of course, this is only because 'is a doctor' is not itself a morally neutral description.

4. There are certainly a number of difficulties with it, as presented here. Note 3 above explains how the is/ought gap might perhaps be closed. It's also objected that Hume is working with an overly narrow conception of what's 'reasonable'. Not everything we call 'reasonable' is either a logical truth, or else justified by means of a deductive or inductive argument. Take, for example, my belief that there is an orange on the table in front of me. It's surely reasonable for me to believe there's an orange on the table. But not because I have *inferred* it's there by means of a cogent argument. I can just *see* it's there. That's why it's reasonable. But if my belief that there's an orange on the table is reasonable despite not being arrived at via a cogent argument, why can't the same be true of my moral beliefs? Why can't I just 'see' that they are true too? After all, 'reason' is also the name of one of our intellectual faculties, alongside our perceptual faculties such as sight and hearing. If the faculty of sight can deliver a reasonable belief without resorting to inference, why can't the faculty of reason?

5. The mechanisms by which natural selection might hardwire us to be moral are well explained by Ridley (1997). For a shorter introduction to this area see Singer (1997: chapter 7).

6. This is not to deny that what motivated these movers and shakers, in the first instance, wasn't just a willingness to apply reason to their existing moral beliefs in a cold, logical, impersonal way. No doubt their feelings also played a role (especially feelings of empathy with and sympathy towards those of another race or sex). But that's not to say reason did not also have an important role to play, particularly (i) in terms of helping them later rationally to justify what they perhaps at first only felt to be true, and (ii) in terms of raising both their intellectual and emotional intelligence (which, as we saw in chapter three, is also something a Liberal, philosophical approach to moral education can facilitate).